Teaching Adult Learners

Teaching Adult Learners

A Guide for Public Librarians

Jessica A. Curtis

LIBRARIES UNLIMITED™

An Imprint of ABC-CLIO, LLC

Santa Barbara, California • Denver, Colorado

Library of Congress Cataloging in Publication Control Number: 2019941120

ISBN: 978-1-4408-6544-2 (paperback)
　　　978-1-4408-6545-9 (ebook)

23 22 21 20 19   1 2 3 4 5

This book is also available as an eBook.

Libraries Unlimited
An Imprint of ABC-CLIO, LLC

ABC-CLIO, LLC
147 Castilian Drive
Santa Barbara, California 93117
www.abc-clio.com

This book is printed on acid-free paper ∞

Manufactured in the United States of America

Contents

Introduction

Who dares to teach must never cease to learn.
> —John Cotton Dana (1856–1929),
> *Respectfully Quoted: A Dictionary*
> *of Quotations* (2010)

Learning can be defined as the purposeful or incidental acquiring of information and skills throughout a person's life that affects his or her life in a cognitive, emotional, and practical way (Jarvis 2018, 25). Why would a book about teaching start with a definition of learning? Because that is the entire point and the goal of all teaching: the people who are being taught learn. While "learning" is often associated with formal institutions and certain periods of life, public libraries are in the forefront of resources and have the capabilities to offer lifelong learning opportunities to adult populations. Librarians and library staff who have an understanding of how and why adults learn can utilize that knowledge to enhance every transaction, from the basic reference interview to formal classes and programs.

The past one hundred years have produced a quantity of valuable research and theories on how adults learn so that instructors can package and present information in a way that increases a person's ability to learn. In its application to the library world, the vast majority of research and literature focuses academic libraries. These works address the particular situations and needs of college students, often focusing on the rising population of nontraditional, or older, students on campus. Adult learning theory and practice as applied to public libraries suffers in comparison to academic libraries in terms of research, textbooks, and professional literature. This work addresses how public libraries can take an active role in learning opportunities for adults. Libraries and their staff can use these theories, practices, and suggestions to maximize library talent and resources to become a recognizable agency of education, assistance, and advocacy to the public.

Library science education has traditionally addressed the teaching aspect of adult reference, adult services, or other adult-oriented degree tracks in terms such as "information literacy," "user education," "bibliographic instruction," and "programming" (ACRL 2016). Some accredited schools are starting to offer course work in instructional design, which is associated with the design, implementation, and evaluation of instructional material. Instructional design, at least in terms of library job titles and descriptions, still applies mainly to an academic setting where instructional design librarians work with faculty to create classes, learning strategies, and online content to connect students with resources in a systematic, practical application of design and learning principles. These same principles and practices are equally applicable in a public library setting, where librarians create guided material for library resources, pathfinders, and other publicly consumed information in addition to reference librarians at the desk, on the phone, virtually, or in classes and programs.

This work is partly a plea and a rationale for accredited library programs to automatically build basic learning theory and instructional design elements into any curriculum track that involves interaction with an adult audience. It is also a demonstration and guide for students and those already in the field of the many ways that librarians can successfully teach individuals in their communities.

BIBLIOGRAPHY

Association of College and Research Libraries (ACRL). 2016. "Library Instruction Courses Offered by Accredited Master's Programs in Library and Information Studies." *Instruction Section Website.* https://acrl.ala.org/IS/instruction-tools-resources-2/professional-development/library-instruction-courses-offered-by-accredited-masters-programs-in-library-and-information-studies/.

Jarvis, Peter. 2018. "Learning to Be a Person in Society: Learning to Be Me." In *Contemporary Theories of Learning: Learning Theorists . . . in Their Own Words*, edited by Knud Illeris. London: Routledge. ProQuest Ebook Central.

Library of Congress, ed. 2010. *Respectfully Quoted: A Dictionary of Quotations*. Mineola, NY: Dover Publications, 337.

ONE

The Growing Role and Impact of Instruction in Public Libraries

Any library staff who work with an adult population can attest to truth of the title of this chapter. There is an increase in the instructive role of public librarians. Not every moment of a reference or technical help interaction is a teaching moment, but it can be argued that most now are, and you want the customer to learn the information and instructions you give. Not only does it fulfill the goal of why they contacted the library but also it adds value to the library in the eyes of that person and the larger community, which is an important consideration in a time when many are questioning the value of physical libraries in a digital age.

U.S. libraries have served as a place for instruction and continuing education since the first private libraries appeared in the eighteenth century. Some of the first libraries centered on private collections that serviced specific populations, such as trade guilds or other special groups, and could be accessed by paying a subscription fee. These libraries not only contained materials that would benefit the group but also served as a congregation and dissemination point for knowledge and experience. Even in its infancy, the U.S. library system "stimulated education and investigation that converged with a developing self-reliance and a sense of independence" (Dawson 2008, 33).

ADDRESSING THE DIGITAL DIVIDE
AND COMMUNITY SUPPORT

Economic disparity, the digital divide, and multiple other factors can put many people in the community at a disadvantage when it comes to how to accomplish now-basic online life tasks, such as paying bills, accessing account information, and navigating healthcare websites (Zickuhr and Smith 2012, 6). The digitization or computer-focused reality of communication and workforce functions also means that those seeking employment are at a disadvantage without basic technical skills and software knowledge. A study on the effect of digitalization in the workforce also shows that those with technical skills can earn more than the national average (Muro et al. 2017, 21). Public libraries are in a unique position to help people of all ages, economic status, and skill levels using library resources, classes and programming, and the ability of the staff to convey information and instruct.

Representative occupations and their digitalization levels

Digital level	Occupation	Digital score	Education requirements	Mean annual wage
High	Software Developers, Applications	94	Bachelor's degree	$104,300
High	Computer Systems Analysts	79	Bachelor's degree	$91,620
High	Financial Managers	61	Advanced degree	$139,720
Medium	Lawyers	58	Advanced degree	$139,880
Medium	Automotive Service Technicians and Mechanics	55	Some college	$41,400
Medium	Registered Nurses	55	Some college	$72,180
Medium	Office Clerks, General	55	Secondary or below	$33,010
Low	Security Guards	31	Secondary or below	$29,730
Low	Cooks, Restaurant	18	Secondary or below	$25,430
Low	Construction Laborers	17	Secondary or below	$37,890
Low	Personal Care Aides	14	Secondary or below	$22,710

Figure 1.1. Representative Occupations and Their Digitalization Levels

Source: Reprinted with permission from Muro, Mark, Sifan Liu, Jacob Whiton, and Siddharth Kulkarni. 2017. *Digitalization and the American Workforce Report*, November 2017; Table 2, p. 12. https://brookings.edu/research/digitalization-and-the-american-workforce.

There are many levels of need in the community. The previous examples highlight those who, without a certain set of information, suffer a distinct detriment in their situation. But what about other groups? Consider local business and entrepreneurs. Often engrossed in all that is entailed in starting or maintaining a business, they may not have the time to explore their local library for tools that can enhance their businesses or ensure their survival. Those who attended business school in the past few decades may have had access to and gained familiarity with resources available to their academic library, such as marketing tools, stocks and business histories, directories, as well as the physical materials in the academic library. That a public library may have access to such tools (if they know they exist in the first place), may not even occur to them. Community outreach, marketing, promotion by library staff, and the physical location of the library go a long way in connecting materials and services to those who need it most in the community.

NAVIGATING THE MODERN LIBRARY

Modern library users have a vast array of old and new resources at their fingertips ranging from books and journals to electronic products and tech resources, but these resources are continually evolving, so there are always new things to learn in order to access them (Ebbitt 2015). Also keep in mind that new library users have to learn to navigate the building and organizational system of a library as well as the online catalog. Then there are the databases and online tools on which the library has spent considerable funds. Buried in websites and seemingly complex at first glance, such resources may be seldom accessed unless the process and the worth are introduced and taught by the librarian. Of course, marketing, signage, and good website design go a long way to connect users to content and services, but invariably, more connections are made with guidance and instruction. Indeed, Michael E. Casey, who coined the phrase "Library 2.0," calls for library staff to "empower library users through participatory, user-driven services," meaning that they have to engage the user and not leave it to chance (Casey and Savastinuk 2007, 5).

The many ways information is stored and accessed means that library staff can only be successful in conveying that information if they are familiar with the product, database, technology, or policy involved with access (Bolton 2016). How can librarians stay up-to-date themselves?

Fortunately, libraries have a built-in ally to user-instruction in the form of library vendors. Many vendors, such as Novelist and EBSCO, spend a substantial amount of time and money training library staff on their products. But, as stated by Joan Ruthven in her study of adult public library users and their use of online resources, "it is important that library staff are adequately trained in the use of online resources in order to be able to assist clients to become self-sufficient and for staff to be able to transfer the skills they have learnt to the client" (Ruthven 2010, 108). Such vendor training for the staff often comes along with the subscription and is available in person upon request or on-demand online. These large entities recognize that staff unfamiliarity with the product means that it is less likely to be "pushed" by the staff to the public and therefore they expend considerable funds toward marketing materials and training to ensure use of their product. Much of such instruction is in fact how to "teach" the same strategies and "how to do" information to the public user.

INFORMATION LITERACY, TECHNOLOGY LITERACY, AND INSTRUCTION

The 2015 ALA president Sari Feldman made a statement in regard to the increasing role of libraries and their staff in how to use technology. "Libraries are not just what we have for people, but what we do for and with people." "Virtually all libraries," she points out, "provide free public access to computer and the internet, wi-fi, technology training and robust digital content that supports education, employment, e-government access and more" (ALA 2015). The library's role in providing access to information is well-known, but now information and technology literacy is a fundamental step in the ability to provide access.

The ALA Presidential Committee on Information Literacy defines the term "information literacy" as the ability "to recognize when information is needed and have the ability to locate, evaluate, and use effectively the needed information" (ALA 2006). As technology and nonprint resources have grown, the ALA updated its competency standards to reflect the growing relationship: "Increasingly, information technology skills are interwoven with, and support, information literacy" (ALA 2007). This means that gaps of knowledge regarding technology fluency increasingly affect a user's information literacy capabilities.

THE REALITIES OF THE PROFESSION

In 2017, a nationwide survey of over 1,100 librarians and library staff asked questions about the connection between the level of instruction or training they had received and the real-world realities of what they were experiencing within their communities (Figure 1.2). Participants were asked if they provide instruction to adults in classes or one-on-one and their level of cognizance that this was, in fact, what the job entailed. The majority responded that they did participate in instruction. They also agreed that formal instruction in how to teach people, either pedagogy or andragogy, would improve their skills and benefit their interactions.

Knowing that instruction or information literacy are an important and growing part of library services, it can be reasoned that a knowledge of instruction and learning theory is integral to information services. If the reader only considers that instruction might be needed in regard to

- Do you have prior education or experience in the field of education (non-library related)?
- Do you provide one-on-one instruction to adults that lasts longer than a traditional reference transaction (Overdrive, Catalog, Databases, Tech Help, etc.)?
- Do you conduct classes in a traditional classroom and/or provide online instruction for adult learners?
- Do you have a Master's in Library Science or Knowledge Management?
- In your graduate program, did you take a specific track of study that meant you would work with adults (not teens or youth)?
- If you do teach or instructed in your position, did you know prior to getting the position that such an activity might be required in the profession?
- Did your library science program offer formal instruction in pedagogy or andragogy?
- Do you believe that formal instruction in how to teach would improve your skills in creating instructional material, classes, and in transmitting information to an adult learner?

Figure 1.2. Teaching and Instruction Survey

electronics inside the library or regarding library materials, consider the following information provided by the Public Library Survey (PLS) of 2016:

- There are 9,057 public libraries in the United States (PLS 8)
- Some 294,216 public access computers are offered through those libraries (PLS 42)
- Public libraries have 391,318,819 electronic books (PLS 60)
- 98.3 percent of material and equipment at public libraries is being accessed (PLS 42)

These figures represent the technology that potentially exists within a public library. It should be noted that it does not reflect programming content, job skills, crafts, parent-teacher instruction, and the myriad of other topics that reflect the instructional wants and needs of individuals and communities all over the country.

The Reference & User Services Association (RUSA), a division of ALA, reflects the increasing role of instruction in the profession by defining reference librarians as ones who "assist, advise, and instruct users in accessing all forms of recorded knowledge. The assistance, advice, and instruction include both direct and indirect service to patrons" (RUSA 2017).

Adult programs, classes, and purposeful instruction vary from library to library. Staffing, staff training and education, community demographics, and even library policy affect the breadth and scope of a library's adult education capabilities. Public libraries can play a pivotal role in the democratic belief that education is an individual right and that education, or learning, can improve the mind (Kranich 2001). Each library proves their worth to the public as a learning hub by taking an active role in the dissemination of information and applicable skills. They can serve a strong community role by being a technology hub and tool-giver, providing what users need when they need it. No matter the situation, whether it is how to work a copy machine or how to add an e-book to a device, adult instruction will occur, and library staff with a basic understanding of how adults learn can positively impact the lives of those in their community.

BIBLIOGRAPHY

American Library Association. 2006. "Presidential Committee on Information Literacy. Final Report." *Advocacy, Legislation & Issues*, July 24, 2006. http://www.ala.org/acrl/publications/whitepapers/presidential. Document ID: 106e5565-9ab9-ad94-8d9f-64962ebcde46.

American Library Association. 2007. "Information Literacy Competency Standards for Higher Education." *Advocacy, Legislation & Issues.* http://www.ala.org/Template.cfm?Section=Home&template=/Con tentManagement/ContentDisplay.cfm&ContentID=33553#iltech.

American Library Association. 2015. "ALA Library Fact Sheet 6." *Public Library Use*, October 2015. http://www.ala.org/tools/libfactsheets/ alalibraryfactsheet06. Document ID: 3e98729c-bcfb-4ff4-d54c-db5 a800b0ce1.

Bolton, Leon. 2016. "Changing Times, Changing Roles." *Libraries Task-force*, December 8, 2016. https://librariestaskforce.blog.gov.uk/2016/ 12/08/changing-times-changing-roles/.

Casey, Michael E., and Laura C. Savastinuk. 2007. *Library 2.0: A Guide to Participatory Library Service.* Medford, NJ: Information Today.

Curtis, Jessica A. 2017. "The Importance of Teaching Adult Librarians How to Teach." *Public Libraries Magazine* 56 (4): 31–33.

Dawson, Robert. 2008. *The Public Library.* New York: Princeton Architectural Press, p. 33.

Ebbitt, Kathleen. 2015. "Five Ways Libraries Are Changing in the Digital Age." *Global Citizen*, January 15, 2015. https://www.globalcitizen. org/en/content/five-ways-libraries-are-changing-in-the-digital-ag/.

Kranich, Nancy. 2001. *Libraries & Democracy: The Cornerstones of Liberty.* Chicago: American Library Association.

Muro, Mark, Sifan Liu, Jacob Whiton, and Siddharth Kulkarni. 2017. *Digitalization and the American Workforce Report*, November 2017. https://www.brookings.edu/research/digitalization-and-the-american-workforce/.

Public Library Survey. 2018. *Fiscal Year 2016 Supplementary Tables.* https://www.imls.gov/sites/default/files/fy2016_pls_tables.pdf.

Reference and User Services Association (RUSA). 2017. "Professional Competencies for Reference and User Services Librarians: RUSA Task Force on Professional Competencies." http://www.ala.org/ rusa/sites/ala.org.rusa/files/content/RUSA%20Professional%20 Competencies%20Final%208-31-2017.pdf.

Ruthven, Joan. 2010. "Training Needs and Preferences of Adult Public Library Clients in the Use of Online Resources." *Australian Library Journal* 59 (3): 108–17. doi:10.1080/00049670.2010.10735996.

Zickuhr, K., and A. Smith. 2012. *Digital Differences.* Washington, DC: Pew Research Center's Internet & American Life Project. http:// pewinternet.org/Reports/2012/Digital-differences.aspx.

TWO

Common Learning Populations and Situations

Libraries are traditionally renowned for holding and making available materials and knowledge to the public, and things inside the library, be they physical or electronic, should reflect the interests and needs of the community they serve. Who are the people or groups in the community that might want, need, or benefit from purposeful learning opportunities at the library? All of the situations in this chapter will have some users who never need a librarian or a staff member to utilize materials or services. But many will. Someone will be stuck and confused, but will never, ever walk up to someone (or call) and ask for help (ask any librarian how many times they've been apologized to for doing their job). Others will be there, on the phone, e-mail, or in the building for that very reason. And they may not expect to need help from the staff (I know how a copier works!) until they suddenly do. Most Americans have the cultural or experiential knowledge that libraries can offer guidance and instruction on their information needs. Whether they know it or not, nearly everyone who comes into the library can be taught a thing or two.

It is the library's responsibility to make sure that there are multiple learning avenues available to those who they serve so as to maximize the library's usefulness to the public. Learning situations for any of the groups listed in this chapter can be either active (one-on-one or class instruction) or passive (books and displays). Any reference transaction becomes an active learning opportunity, sometimes referred to as "bibliographic instruction," when the librarian takes the time to show the patron how to find the information or perform an action themselves rather than just giving it or doing it for them (Cooke 2010, 215–17). This can happen in person or virtually, but it does require a conversation to happen between the librarian and the patron. Passive learning lends itself to more opportunities because it can reach more people (i.e., everyone who does not come and talk to staff). This can include strategically placed material like posters, bookmarks, handouts, or other ephemera near certain library sections. This kind of material can be dropped at off-site locations where people can still benefit from the information. Individuals will have definite preferences on how they would normally like to receive information and instruction though circumstances will often force their hand as to which method they ultimately use.

RECREATIONAL READERS

Recreational readers, pleasure readers, book enthusiasts, or whatever you call them are one of the most well-known user groups in a public library. All librarians know of those book-lovers who come in regularly to search for a new find, to reread their beloved favorites, or just because their thirst for new reads can never be quenched. Library workers themselves often fit into this category. Book-lovers are the most common group to ask the basic readers' advisory question "Can you recommend a good book?."

Active Learning Scenarios

There are many print and online sources to help the librarian (and the patron) in finding the elusive "perfect read." Have the patron be the one to search the resource, such as the readers' advisory database NoveList or the library's own links for recommendations, talking them through the steps until they get the result they want. Some may want to watch you do it first. If that's the case, make sure that they try it themselves after you, so that they know they can do it. This creates multiple points of exercise and memory that patrons can tap into the next time they want a recommendation.

Passive Learning Scenarios

Bookmarks placed in best sellers with clear visuals and instructions on one side and a list of read-alikes for that title, author, or genre are a good way to "go to where the people are." Some library catalogs integrate with popular websites and services, such as GoodReads.com to offer suggestions whenever someone searches the catalog. Quick GIF tutorials embedded on the website, simply showing people how to navigate and search resources, are a quick fix for those who might not have been aware of the resource.

TECHNOLOGY USERS

Either by choice or by circumstance, libraries serve as a technology hub for many Americans. This is where they go to access and get help with computers, Wi-Fi, fax machines, printers, and even older technology that may be hard to find in stores like typewriters and floppy drives. Users may come and go and not need assistance (I know how a copier works!), but many will need to be walked through unfamiliar equipment and processes to get to the end that they need. Others may actually have all they need at home but want the "backup" of the technical assistance they receive at the library.

Libraries around the country offer classes and programming surrounding new devices, such as smartphones, e-readers, tablets, software, and even operating systems. Even if a library doesn't offer a specific class, most will guide, assist, and instruct those who walk in with a question about a device. Fear is a common factor for many of those seeking help with these expensive items (often gifted by a well-meaning family member) and cultural saturation has made them feel like they "should already know" how to work them (McDonough 2016, 2). Patience and a realization of how fast technology has changed for many in the community will help the librarian overcome the "fear" so that patrons can begin to learn. Their learning opens them to the possibility of being self-sufficient and adds value to their original purpose.

Active Learning Scenarios

Individuals using the library's tech resources will frequently engage nearby staff to help with their need or project. It is important to conduct a proper reference interview to ascertain the user's actual need, since if they are unfamiliar with technological terms, they may not know how to explain their need (Ohio Reference Excellence, Module 2, n.d.). Time, energy, and seating room in classes may be saved if their question can be answered on the spot. Classes on software applications (e.g., Microsoft Word), common computing systems (e.g., Windows 10), or social media sites (e.g., Facebook) are popular with multiple user groups.

Passive Learning Scenarios

Those who help with technology in the library can tell you that the same questions get asked over and over. The library can post these FAQs and their answers where the questions commonly occur. This may mean listing the steps above a copier or fax, or recording instructional GIFs to put on the desktops of public access computers. Libraries can accommodate those who don't attend the in-person classes by recording them and making the videos available on the library website or social media sites. Making class handouts and any tech instruction sheets (e.g., how to download e-books) available online and on the floor at the library can reach those who may not even know that the class exists.

LIFELONG LEARNERS

This group actively wants to *know* and to *understand*, which almost always makes things easier for the learner and the teacher. They are not necessarily motivated by an explicit need but more by interest and curiosity. For hobbyists, amateur historians, and those who are interested in self-improvement, there are materials in every part of the library that may spark their interest. That being said, they may not be *in* the library. Search the community for hobby stores or local interest groups (often found at Meetup.com or Facebook). This will tell the library who is there and what their interests are.

Active Learning Scenarios

Many in this group are familiar faces to staff, since they already sign up for a variety of library classes and programs. Advertising to specific groups outside the library, especially something that teaches them more about their personal (hard to find experts in) interest, can be an effective way to draw in new library users. For example, one library in Ohio had a very large crowd, many exclaiming that they hadn't been in a library for years, come in to hear a model train expert teach enthusiasts how to get started making a backyard setup. Lifelong learners are one of the easiest groups for whom to recommend a transition from fiction to nonfiction so they can learn more about the subject ("If you liked *Pompeii* by Robert Harris you might like *Krakatoa* by Simon Winchester"). Demonstrating new library products, new databases, and new technology can become an "easy sell" to these interested individuals. This group can be generous and effusive if surveyed for new program ideas; the library simply has to ask the public what they want.

Passive Learning Scenarios

Lifelong learners have been known to inspect any new display out of sheer interest. Recommended reading lists, book displays, handouts, and instructions meant for specific user groups may still draw in the lifelong learner. Well-designed websites and catalogs can draw someone looking for a particular book to a website, to a class, or to a program.

INSTRUCTION AND INFORMATION SEEKERS

Certain situations call for specific informational needs. Individuals often need to learn computer programs for work, such as spreadsheets, e-mail systems, or word processing applications in order to do their jobs. Someone may need language books or language translator apps to get ready for their overseas vacation. Someone is diagnosed with an illness or someone with no money for a plumber has a flooded basement; there are as many potential situations as there are people. Those with an explicit need may be lifelong learners and already be familiar with the fact that the library houses the answer to their need. Others come to the library because they were sent there by someone else ("I think the library can help you"). This group often has a need for information *right now* and may therefore not be as open to a "teachable moment." Others take time and make a concerted effort to learn and fulfill their need. The immediacy of their need and their own personal ability dictate how much instruction they need or want. Instructor beware; there may be high emotion and impatience if the need is *very* immediate and they need help ("How does this machine work?! I need to fax this in the next ten minutes!").

Active Learning Scenarios

Any program or class that teaches someone how to perform a task and get an end result, such as gardening, knitting, test prep, or how to get your book published, are a means of fulfilling someone's specific need. The attendees to these kinds of classes will have specific information goals so they can perform *their* goals. Besides addressing common tech situations ("I need to print my resume for an interview in twenty minutes and it's on my phone!"), librarians can teach individuals how to find materials, databases, outside resources, and even online tutorials that may address their needs.

Passive Learning Scenarios

If someone who hasn't been in the library for ten years comes in to grab a book on estate planning, are they aware of the library's free legal form database that has thirty different last will and testament templates? Do they know that the library offers free notary services or that there is a free legal clinic held there once a month? This scenario can play out with a variety of topics. Placing signage and brochures in the stacks beside relevant material may be the best way in some cases to inform the grab-and-go patron. Having similar material and links come up when certain keywords are entered in the catalog can help both the librarian and the user. The library can post small ads to this effect on their social media sites, such as "Doing some DIY? We can help," as a reminder that the library has materials that can help patrons with their next project. Book displays that focus on common needs, such as retirement, computer skills, and job seeking, are another way to appeal to those who might not have thought of the library to address their needs.

ADULT STUDENTS

Adult students refer to college-aged or nontraditional students (Cooke 2010, 211). This group often uses the public library for the tables, quiet spaces, computers, printers, and free Wi-Fi and may not interact much with the staff or library content. Their educational institutions may have their own libraries and resources, but the students are at the public library either because the public library is more convenient or because they are online students. Online students may not be familiar at all with their institution's library or online resources, if their school even has them. This person may be in the library primarily for the space and Wi-Fi, but the library will often have resources that will help them in their academic studies.

Active Learning Scenarios

These individuals may be in the library several times a week and never interact with staff. A librarian who is attentive and interested in patrons can go a long way in helping these busy, and often stressed, students. Are they holding an anatomy book and wearing scrubs? Ask them if they're in medical school. Did they know about the journal database that they can use for their next paper that cites things automatically? Did they know they can have free Microsoft Word through OneDrive.com to write papers? Do they know how to order textbooks through your interlibrary loan system? Tell them what the library has to help them. Show them where to find it. Then teach them how to do it. Classes or programs labeled specifically for adult students (e.g., GRE Prep class or Research Tips for Online Students) can draw in those who you don't reach one-on-one.

Passive Learning Scenarios

If they're using the tables, take the instruction to the tables. Tabletop displays, like a plastic menu holder in a restaurant, can give 1–2–3 instructions on how to access library research materials or remind them how to cite a page in a popular paper format. Book, brochure, and information displays near study areas can make them aware of in-house materials that can help them study for licensing tests (e.g., NCLEX) or help them with their research (e.g., APA Style Guide).

BUSINESSES AND ENTREPRENEURS

This is a highly interested and invested group as long as they know it will benefit their time and bottom-line. Some business owners have been in business so long that they predate a number of print and online resources that exist primarily for them, meaning that they don't even know that they exist. New entrepreneurs can almost be overwhelmed at the amount of information. Another group of online entrepreneurs may be using the library facilities, not interacting with staff, and not realize the potential tools the library owns.

There are a variety of materials commonly held by libraries that may be too expensive for a small business to acquire on their own. These may include publications (e.g., Forbes Magazine), print or online directories for supplies or manufacturing companies (e.g., Manufacturing & Distribution U.S.A.), online training databases (e.g., LearningExpress Library), and other databases geared toward business and marketing research (e.g., ReferencesUSA). Marketing material may have to be specifically targeted in order to reach and educate this group, partially due to the long hours associated with owning your own business.

Active Learning Scenarios

Actively engage the person who runs their business from the library. They may be at the library every day and can be differentiated from the student by the material they use as well as the phone calls they take and place throughout the day. Schedule a time to speak at a local business association meeting or at the local chamber of commerce meetings. Make an appointment with individual, non-chain-store owners or just stop in and introduce yourself. Have a packet of information that is specifically targeted toward their business interests. Find out about business conferences that might be held near the library and get a table at the expo halls. Offer classes specifically targeted toward business owners or office managers (e.g., "Marketing your business with A to Z Database").

Passive Learning Scenarios

Circulate those reference books! Especially if the same information is available online or in a library database. Prepackage instructions on how to use databases to make the connection between the service and their businesses abundantly clear. Place displays in high-traffic areas not normally associated with adult nonfiction or business materials. Send an introduction letter along with at least one applicable database or event guide to businesses designated as "home based" in the community.

NEW ADULTS

The term "new adults," coined by St. Martin's Press in 2009 for those between the ages of nineteen and twenty-five, is often associated with targeting readers of genre fiction (Cart 2016, 143). It has grown to mean library users who straddle the line between adolescent and adult interests. And it's not just about their reading tastes. From paying their own bills, cooking solo, to sewing a button, there are many new adults who are using the library to bolster their life skills. Libraries around the country that host "Adulting 101" classes are inundated by the interested (Ford 2018). This wave is helping a new generation learn the informative and instructive capabilities of the public library (without their parents).

Active Learning Scenarios

Libraries that already host programs for college-bound teens have a built-in audience for subjects that might appeal to "new adults." Libraries located in college towns can take advantage of campus activities that draw in large crowds to highlight classes and resources or even to teach something useful on the spot. Partnering with student service offices can help identify needs and interests that the academic side is unable to fulfill. Don't forget about the restaurants and bars! Mini demonstrations, classes on-site, or a rollicking trivia night can make people aware of library resources and aides.

Passive Learning Scenarios

This is an online generation, so put it online! Create a channel on YouTube, Vemo, or other online video sites to catch those who are used to going online for all their answers. Attach materials, links to video tutorials, a PDF of instructions, or other how-tos to common subjects, searches, and keywords. Make displays of "adult" material in the library areas that are frequented by this population. Have "off-site libraries" in the form of bookshelves or brochure stands at local establishments that cater to the age group.

PARENTS AND TEACHERS

Parents and teachers are often not in the library for themselves but for their children and students. Any youth or teen librarian can tell you though that their spiel on a database or how to find a lexicon level is directed to the adult. Besides accessing materials and resources for the children, this group may not be aware of the multitude of resources available *for* them *about* their kids.

There are many reasons why parents of young children may visit only the media or children's section of a library. Parents, identified by the ALA as a child's first teacher, may be in the library for story time, to get books for their kids, or to help them with schoolwork (ALA 2017, 1). Having small children may mean that parents either accidently or purposefully avoid the adult area because of their children's potential decibel level or sheer busyness.

Active Learning Scenarios

Events for young children (should) always mean that for each child there is an adult with them, or at least nearby. Short demonstrations, either while they're waiting or as part of a program at the beginning or end, on how to find or use materials that are pertinent to them can help fill a needed information gap. Teachers may not be aware of databases, parent-teacher sections, interlibrary loan opportunities, or that the library can make classroom visits. Again, the reference interview is a great way to find out what they need and what they do or don't know about what the library has to offer.

Passive Learning Scenarios

A strategically placed cart of books near children's programs on potty training, how to get your child to sleep, along with a multitude of other subjects normally found in the adult section can be an enlightening boon to busy parents. Place signage or instructions in the children's section to remind parents and teachers about the material meant for adult readers on the same topic. Create links and text boxes on the website attached to certain keywords or materials meant to catch the adult eye.

OLDER ADULTS

While each generation or age group has their own common needs and concerns, an aging population may start to deal with new issues that challenge their normal experiences and potentially their ability to learn. Although not true for all, common issues may include a change in vision (e.g., large print needs), a change in mobility (e.g., a need for outreach services), or sudden changes in life situations (e.g., retirement or death of a spouse). Add in the way technology is continually changing the basics of everyday life and communication and you have a built-in population for a multitude of library classes, workshops, and one-on-ones.

Active Learning Scenarios

Offer assistance to those in the building who are obviously struggling with something. They may not know that the library is capable of helping. Build in classes to Outreach services that visit local retirement homes or senior centers featuring common device issues, library e-material how-tos, or other senior-appropriate class content. Market senior-specific classes at the library and one-on-one tutorials, especially after major gift-giving holidays. Coordinate demonstrations at local electronic stores to educate users in how to get and use free library material with their devices. Bring in professionals to speak on large issues that might interest this population such as Medicare, Social Security, voting issues, and downsizing.

Passive Learning Scenarios

Leave detailed instructions regarding library services and material in areas frequented by this demographic. In some libraries this might mean the library coffee shop or the library meeting room where their local club or hobbyist group meets every week. Make an area for those who still prefer print that contains large print (LP) class handouts and instructions on a variety of topics (e.g., "How to Navigate Obamacare" or "FaceTime 101"). Create displays of books and other resources that feature senior-specific materials (e.g., *Windows 10 for Seniors*).

JOB SEEKERS

Job seekers are either in need of a job because they don't have one or because they want to leave the one they currently have. If times are tight because of their situation they may end up at the library for Wi-Fi use, online job searching, printing resumes, or to find the latest book on interview tips. Finding a job may mean learning a new skill ("Everyone wants you to know Word!") or navigating the online job application world ("What happened to dropping off my resume with HR?"). Library resources and staff can make a monumental difference in this potentially stressful transition in someone's life (Gutsche 2011, 28–31).

Active Learning Scenarios

Coordinate with local employment centers to give off-site classes on common skills that employers desire. Give workshops, programs, and classes at the library marketed specifically to job seekers such as "Soft Skills Every Employer Wants" or "Resume Review" sessions. Actively approach those looking at job sites or working on resumes and let them know what the library has that might help them.

Passive Learning Scenarios

Post vetted job search websites and search strategies beside library computers as well as on the library website and on paper, such as bookmarks. Leave this material, as well as any other instructional material, on skill-building databases such as Lynda.com or LearningExpress Library at local employment centers. Create folders or direct links to job sites and resume templates on the desktops of library computers.

Being aware of the users in the community and what they might need is only half the battle. Librarians have to make the effort to engage, either actively or passively, with those populations. When they do, not only does it satisfy an immediate want or need but also helps to build information literacy skills and personal confidence in the individual.

BIBLIOGRAPHY

Advocacy. 2017. *From Baby's First Words: Libraries Promote Early Learning*, January 17. American Library Association. http://www.ala.org/advocacy/sites/ala.org.advocacy/files/content/access/Early_childhood_A-WEB_01-17-17.pdf.

Cart, Michael. 2016. *Young Adult Literature: From Romance to Realism.* Chicago: Neal-Schuman, an Imprint of the American Library Association.

Cooke, Nicole. 2010. "Becoming an Andragogical Librarian: Using Library Instruction as a Tool to Combat Library Anxiety and Empower

Adult Learners." *New Review of Academic Librarianship* 16 (2): 208–227.

Ford, Anne. 2018. "Adulting 101: When Libraries Teach Basic Life Skills." *American Libraries Magazine*, April 23, 2018. https://americanlibraries magazine.org/2018/05/01/adulting-101-library-programming/.

Gutsche, Betha. 2011. "A Boon to the Workforce." *Library Journal*, September 1, 2011.

Marks, Gene. 2018. "Love You, Mom: Report Predicts Near-Record Mother's Day Sales." *Chicago Tribune*, April 26, 2018. http://www. chicagotribune.com/business/ct-biz-mothers-day-sales-20180426-story.html.

McDonough, Carol C. 2016. "The Effect of Ageism on the Digital Divide among Older Adults." *Journal of Gerontology and Geriatric Medicine* 2: 008.1. http://heraldopenaccess.us/fulltext/Gerontology-&-Geriatric-Medicine/The-Effect-of-Ageism-on-the-Digital-Divide-Among-Older-Adults.pdf.

Ohio Reference Excellence. n.d. "Module 2: The Reference Interview." http://oreonline.olc.org/modules/module-2-reference-interview/.

Weverka, Peter. 2018. *Windows 10 for Seniors for Dummies*. Hoboken, NJ: John Wiley.

THREE

An Introduction to Andragogy

In its simplest terms, andragogy is the art and science of teaching adults. Adults are complex creatures who differ as much individually as they do across age, national, or cultural boundaries. There are a variety of theories that attempt to uncover and explain the particular needs of adult learners. Two models in particular, Maslow's Hierarchy of Needs (1943) and Knowles's Assumptions of Adult Learners (1984), can provide insight about the basic motivations of most adults who are seeking instruction. This information can help library staff when planning classes, marketing, and general learning situations so that those seeking instruction can get the most out of the interaction.

MASLOW'S HIERARCHY OF NEEDS

Maslow's model, first introduced in 1943, states that humans have external and internal motivators for everything that they do and that they're geared to satisfy the most basic needs like food, shelter, and safety first (370–378). Next are the psychological needs of relationships and self-esteem; then come curiosity and self-actualization. Each person has his or her own fluid order of priorities (e.g., someone takes money out of the food budget to get the latest phone), but libraries may see two specific scenarios play out in regard to people coming to the library for instruction (Fradera 2018, 14).

First, if learning something can help fulfill a basic need, then its value is inherently obvious and the person will be highly motivated to come and learn. Job help, food stamp information, legal clinics, healthcare information; these are all primary examples that can affect everyday life of individuals and families. Threats or problems, whether physical or mental, that involve relationships and personal emotions will also motivate people to address the situation (if I want to talk to my grandkids, I'm going to have to learn to text!). If they recognize the need for the information and skill, they will endure discomfort and potential trials to get the help they need. On the other hand, if any of the "more important" items in the hierarchy would have to be sacrificed in order to come to the library for help, it's not going to happen.

Most librarians have had the experience where they have identified the need and have the *perfect program* that will really make a difference to those in their community . . . and the attendance is awful. There may be good reasons, according to Maslow, that have direct applications for public libraries and may help explain class statistics and program demographics. Someone wants to attend a library class that only happens at night because the information might be useful at work, but there's no babysitter or there's no transportation or they don't feel safe in that part of town at night. Another person works second shift and weekends and can't get off work for any evening class. Someone else only has one obligation-free afternoon and that's the only time to catch up on housework. Any or all of these things mean that the person is not likely to come, even if the program is everything they ever needed.

Libraries can help motivate users to come to the library by helping them rationalize the instruction as a greater need that will improve other things in their lives and by addressing potential roadblocks to their attendance. Marketing and conversations between the staff and the patrons can draw the lines between library instruction opportunities and personal (e.g., save money), professional (e.g., get a job), and educational (e.g., free textbooks) benefits that may speak to primary needs. Varying class times, from morning to evening or weekdays to weekends, may accommodate the needs of those with time restrictions. Hosting classes off-site at businesses, community centers, or near transportation hubs may help those with transportation issues. If patrons say that they can't come, especially if they exhibited interest, ask why (generally) or ask what would enable them to come. The answers may help pinpoint ways the library can reach those who really need what they're offering.

KNOWLES'S ASSUMPTIONS OF ADULT LEARNERS

Malcolm Shephard Knowles popularized the term "andragogy" in the 1970s and 1980s with a series of papers addressing the specific teaching and learning needs of adult learners (Merriam and Bierema 2014, 44–46). These are assumptions from the viewpoint of the teacher.

The Six Assumptions of Adult Learners

1. Adults are self-directed.
2. Personal experiences are a resource when learning and can affect how someone learns.
3. An adult becomes increasingly willing or ready to learn when the outcome has a personal or social consequence.
4. The purpose of learning is to fix a want or need and the outcomes of learning should be immediately applicable.
5. An adult's motivation to learn is internal instead of external.
6. There has to be a reason to learn something new. (Knowles 1984, 12)

Acknowledging that these are factors in those who seek instruction at the library can affect both the experience and outcome for the student as well as the instructor.

Self-Directed

Treating adults as though they are self-directed means realizing that they are making the effort by their own volition. They are in that situation because they choose to be there. Moreover, they've chosen the library as their resource when they could have paid for the privilege at another institution or tried it alone. It also means that whether they actually learn the material is their responsibility. This doesn't mean that the instructor has no effect on what they are learning, but the ultimate outcome, their follow-through, information-seeking behavior, and retention is mainly a matter of their own personal efforts.

Personal Experience

The second principle, that personal experiences affect how someone learns, means that no one is a blank slate when he or she comes into the library. They may be absolute beginners in whatever subject they're addressing, but something else they know may pertain to it and they just hadn't made the connection. Ignoring the content or value of what someone knows or has experienced can make a person feel discounted or devalued (Merriam and Bierema 2014, 50). It may also mean that people may have to overcome their own experiences or unlearn something in order to learn something new. An example of this would be those who come to an Android Smartphone class meant for beginners. They have had a smartphone before, but it was a different operating system and they are having trouble adapting to their new phone so they are attending the class. They will be ahead of the class in terms of concepts (apps, texting, and touchscreens) but are getting stuck on the differences in appearance, location, and workflow. Everyone there may define themselves as a "beginner," but their previous experiences mean that people are going to learn at different rates and have feelings or beliefs about their capabilities and skill levels.

Readiness to Learn and Applicability

Most adults who seek instruction or evince a readiness to learn are doing so because they need to know or do something. This need means that they are increasingly willing to spend time and effort, both expensive commodities to adults, if it has a beneficial payoff. Many may come to the library specifically expecting help to be there in terms of either material or services. The increasing variety of potential instruction-seeking groups as listed in Chapter 2 demonstrates that many of the learning opportunities can point to a clear resolution of an immediate need. This applicability of instruction is a continual selling point for successful adult learning opportunities at libraries. The "students" tell others, share experiences, and come back for more.

Motivating Factors

Most adults have at some point put something off that they needed to do or learn that they considered boring or uninteresting. Then a deadline, a boss, a job opportunity, or something that could result in a consequence (good or bad) makes that learning now a problem-solving endeavor. Information may be "interesting," but fulfilling that "want" or internally motivated task, according to Maslow's hierarchy, will usually occur after the other basic needs are fulfilled. An example of this for an adult program would be someone choosing to take a spreadsheet class because he or she needs it for work over a crafting class that would be taken for fun. External motivators are when the "reason" is because they can't get out of it (often in seen in library programs when a spouse unwillingly attends). External motivators can become internal when people agree as to why they need the information or skill. Good instructors can help bridge the gap between the two and help people make personal, internally motivating applications that help the instruction stick.

ANDRAGOGY IN THE LIBRARY

A multi-person class cannot usually teach to just one person's needs, but clarity in program descriptions can help make sure that those who sign up know that some aspect of the class is directed toward their particular issue. Below is a look at the reasons each person in an adult Facebook 101 class is attending the class. They are all exhibiting self-directed behavior and a readiness to learn because they are there in the seats.

	Reason for Attending	**Motivators and Learning Factors**
Person #1	Facebook is the only way he can see his family's pictures. His family tends to do it for him instead of teaching him.	Emotional needs, social pressure, self-worth
Person #2	Got a tablet when the computer died and the difference between the online Facebook and the mobile version is stopping her from using it. She was a heavy user and friends and family are worriedly starting to contact her via other methods.	Personal experience, self-worth, emotional needs, social pressure
Person #3	Wants to learn how to use Facebook for her business. She has an account, but has never used it.	Basic professional need, marketing and money consequences
Person #4	Doesn't want everyone to see his posts and wants to completely block certain people from his account.	Emotional needs, personal experience, social consequence

All of the students signed up for a two-hour basic class that explicitly listed what the class would contain: a review of the website and the mobile app on how to post, find friends and their content, upload pictures, adjust privacy settings, and how to send personal messages. The instructor is not privy to why people want to attend before they come, so the instructor assumes that they want to learn one or all of the things that were listed in the description. There are some who are not "beginners" but will still benefit from the experience because the class addresses some aspect of their needs. The class does, in fact, address some aspect of every attendee's reason for attending. The only one who isn't having her primary need filled (the business owner) is still getting what she needs, if not what she exactly wanted, because she was not familiar with the fundamentals of Facebook use.

The number of people involved in a learning situation will affect the extent to which the instructor can address an individual's exact learning goal. One-on-one sessions regularly allow for immediate problem-solving lessons (e.g., "click here to access their pictures"). Small classes offer the opportunity for instructors to ask why people are there and directly apply the general class information to their particular reason for attending (e.g., "this setting will allow you to be 'friends only', so everyone can't see your posts"). This can sometimes be done in larger classes as well but instead leads to generalizations or addressing the most commonly held questions.

Instruction is now an integral part of most adult librarian positions. An understanding of andragogy and adult learners can give librarians and any staff who give instruction a basic frame of reference concerning those they are seeking to help. Communication with patrons is the only way that librarians will know the reasons and motivations for why someone is coming to the library for help. Their internal and external motivations, their circumstances and personal priorities, and their own interests and capabilities will play a larger part in getting people into the library than any marketing endeavor. By addressing common barriers such as transportation, varying class times, or directly correlating classes and services with important outcomes (e.g., save money or get a job), libraries have a greater chance to reach those who genuinely need a helping hand.

BIBLIOGRAPHY

"Andragogy." *Merriam-Webster.* https://www.merriam-webster.com/dictionary/andragogy.

Fradera, Alex. 2018. "Maslow—Putting the Record Straight." *Psychologist*, August 2018, 13–14. https://proxy.library.kent.edu/login.

Groves, D. L., Harvey Kahalas, and David L. Erickson. 1975. "A Suggested Modification to Maslow's Need Hierarchy." *Social Behav-*

ior & Personality: An International Journal 3 (1): 65–69. doi:10.
2224/sbp.1975.3.1.65.

Knowles, Malcolm S. 1980. *The Modern Practice of Adult Education: From Pedagogy to Andragogy.* New York: Cambridge Books.

Knowles, Malcolm S. 1984. *Andragogy in Action: Applying Modern Principles of Adult Learning.* San Francisco: Jossey-Bass.

Knowles, Malcolm S. 1986. *The Adult Learner: A Neglected Species.* Houston: Gulf. https://files.eric.ed.gov/fulltext/ED084368.pdf.

Maslow, A. H. 1943. "A Theory of Human Motivation." *Psychological Review* 50 (4): 370–396.

Merriam, Sharan B., and Laura L. Bierema. 2014. *Adult Learning: Linking Theory and Practice.* San Francisco: Jossey-Bass.

FOUR

Generational Learning Considerations

Any theory or consideration that organizes people into different groups does so in an effort to discern patterns that help explain behaviors and attitudes. In learning theories, such as when applied to generations, it is meant to help instructors and institutions arrange and present information in a way that best helps an individual learn. Generational learning theories assume that those born in a certain range of time, or generational cohorts, share similar historical and social experiences (Pilcher 1994, 481–84). These contexts can create differences from one generation to the next in how individuals interact with and view instruction, teachers, other students, and feedback. (Take care to treat the attributes in this chapter as generalizations, as individuals may not conform to specific generational traits.)

GENERATIONAL LEARNING ATTRIBUTES

Generation titles were first introduced as an American concept after the baby boomers born between 1946 and 1964 came onto the scene after World War II. According to a 2018 Pew Research report, there are at least five adult generations that libraries are likely to encounter, either as employees or as patrons (Dimock 2019). The Silent, or Greatest Generation, the parents of the baby boomers, was born before 1945. Generation X was born between 1965 and 1980. Millennials, or Generation Y, were born between 1981 and 1996 and now, according to the Pew study, make up the majority of the American workforce. The oldest Post-Millennials, some-times called Generation Z, born after 1997, are already twenty-one and competing for jobs. Beyond the labels, these are members of every community and user group that the library tries to serve. So, what are the characteristics of the different generations in regards to learning?

The Silent Generation (Pre–1945)

Members of the Silent Generation grew up during the Great Depression and World War II and are the parents of the Baby Boomers. They are often patriotic, hard-working, and traditionalist in terms of family roles. They experienced rapid social and technological changes throughout their lives and tend to be loyal to employers. This generation, the wealthiest in American history, now has one of the largest lobbying agencies, the AARP, representing their interests in consumer needs, healthcare, and politics (Morris 1996, 4). Despite their dwindling numbers, they commonly make up the majority of voters for any given election, local or national, making them incredibly influential to library organizations that rely on voters for funding (Fry 2018).

The Silent Generation members, as traditionalists, value organization, formality, and authority in a learning situation (Zemke et al. 1999). They view the presenter or teacher as an authority figure and expect to learn the purpose or application of the topic or material. The appearance and speaking ability of the instructor, as well as the grammar and mechanics of written material, will either enhance or invalidate the learning experience.

Baby Boomers (1946–1964)

Boomers were born in the heyday of American prosperity and productivity. They were the largest generation that America had ever seen and were the driving force behind racial and cultural revolutions. Marketers taught them that, as the largest segment of the population, their needs, interests, and wants were to be attended to. This was the first generation where college was a readily acceptable goal for both men and women. They came of age along with world-changing technology (they used the first computers) that they applied in everyday life and work. They were taught, and experienced, that education and hard work would pay off in acquiring the American dream. Many are greatly aware of the information or technology gap that might exist between them and younger generations, but they believe that they are capable of learning. The retirement age is getting older (sixty-six according to the Social Security Administration at the time this was written), and these skill gaps will drive information-seeking behavior (Social Security, n.d.).

Boomers are likely to seek instruction for skill-building, problem-solving, and general interests, since they attribute value to education and the expertise granted by a teacher. They have good social skills and value politeness and affability from instructors and other participants. Having their skills and experience acknowledged is important to build rapport and respect. In a classroom, this may translate to asking participants to share what they already know or what they like about the subject. Boomers appreciate organized information, which may mean a highly structured presentation of information, a regimented class experience, or that class handouts and any takeaway material are well-formulated. This group, according to Coates in her book *Generational Learning Styles*, likes to be treated like they're young (2007, 88). Any treatment, even if it's well-meant, that indicates that they are in any way "old" with likely alienate participants and cause them to disengage with the instruction.

Generation X (1965–1980)

Those in Generation X, or GenX, had a different worldview and expectations than those before them thanks to historical and economic events in their lifetimes. They tend to be family-oriented, pragmatic, independent, and view the world as unreliable. In a learning situation, this means that a class that competes with family needs is going to fare badly. It also means that class information should be clear, to the point, and immediately applicable. GenX is a proponent of using humor as a problem-solving tool and as a means of engagement, meaning that they appreciate the use of humor in learning situations. Traditionally labeled as "unmotivated" learners, active learning and highly visual materials can help keep them engaged with the material. That being said, research has proven that this generation of students stays more engaged and better retains material if given in fifteen- to twenty-minute chunks followed by an activity that uses the information (Noel 2016, 14).

Millennials (1981–1996)

Millennials are the most highly studied of the generations to date and as of 2018 make up the majority of the U.S. workforce. They are the first to be considered "digital natives" and the first to have lived their entire lives "connected" in some way to technology (Prensky 2001). Most are assumed to be technically literate and able to multi-task with ease. In an instructional setting, this means that they expect the use of technology or expect the information to be available away from the physical library. They appreciate clear goals and instructions, proven experts, positive feedback, and group interactions (Nikischer 2017, 2). Other important factors that help engage Millennials are the use of activities instead of lectures, making content relevant to their lives, a relaxed learning environment, and a good relationship with the instructor (Barton 2011).

Post-Millennials or Generation Z (1997–Present)

This generation is now entering college and the workforce and therefore needs to be considered when addressing adult education needs. While all the generations so far mentioned have had the shared experience of the Internet, smartphones, and Google, they had all also experienced a world that didn't contain them. Conversely, no member of Generation Z has lived in a world without these tools. Information has always been available 24/7 to this group, so they are more likely than any other group to rely on self-instruction. Online, self-guided courses and short instruction videos are preferred over traditional classroom settings. Getting this group in the building will mean proving to them that the librarian, the library resources, and any kind of class has more value than something that they can find online. This means marketing by more modern means (i.e., social media and online radio) to connect with them in the first place and making the relationship between them and the information "personal, relevant, and long-lasting" (Mohr and Mohr 2017, 91).

AGE-SPECIFIC CONSIDERATIONS

Libraries around the country offer classes and programs in addition to the on-demand help, on a variety of topics to all ages. Despite not being meant for a specific age group, certain factors often contribute to a skewed attendance demographic. Some common life experiences start to be generation-specific (with the occasional outlier) such as child-rearing, adulting skills, taking care of aging parents, retirement, and certain health issues.

Marketing and program-title considerations, such as labeling a class for parents, seniors, new graduates, or grandparents, are also a reliable way of purposely building a class made predominantly of a specific generation. Knowing that is most likely to happen in such situations, the instructor can tailor the class to that generation's common learning preferences.

Timing also plays a large part in which age demographic attends a class or when they come in to the library for assistance. Older generations with mobility or eyesight issues or for considerations of safety will favor day-time classes and interactions. The same though is true for retirees, shift workers, the unemployed, and stay-at-home parents. Work and family considerations might mean that others are only available on the weekends or some evening hours. It's important to consider the intended audience and make sure that library offerings are available when they are.

TEACHING TO DIVERSITY

Generational differences and preferences may make the idea of teaching to a mixed generation group a daunting task. But there are ways to plan instruction to a diverse community, especially when there is no way to determine who (age-wise) will attend the class or seek instruction. Here are some basic strategies that speak to all generations.

Space and Tools

Although taking away tables will allow for more chairs (a.k.a. attendees), do consider a table and chair setup for most programming needs, including lecture situations. Tables allow those with compromised motor skills or balance the ability to brace themselves and their devices. Even if someone doesn't have physical issues, it offers a stable platform for note-taking and general comfort. If tables seriously impact the potential size of participation, consider creating a mix of table seating and chairs. Ambient noise and lighting should also be taken into consideration in a teaching space. Eyesight and hearing problems know no age limit and one bad class can prevent someone from coming back.

Assume Interest

Some stereotypes suggest that only people of a certain age will seek certain forms of instruction. The truth is: need, interest, ability, and opportunity are more the motivators than age. If they are in the physical library or accessing instructional materials through the library website, they are already demonstrating interest and a motivation to learn.

Be Personable

All generations want to connect to the instructor in some manner, whether they consider them an authority figure or a peer. In person, this means showing interest in them as people, asking questions and inviting comments, and being generally polite and friendly. Online, this means making sure that recorded material is upbeat and engaging and speaks directly to the learner.

Show Some Respect

Everyone wants to be respected. This may look like different things to different generations, but in general, it means acknowledging an individual's previous accomplishments and knowledge. One-on-one, it can also mean giving specific time and attention to the learner. In a classroom, it can mean making sure that things run on time and that distractions and disturbances are addressed.

Subject Authority

People like their instructors to be "experts." Whether it's through credentials, years of experience, or demonstrated competence, they have more trust in the teacher and a feeling of ease with the subject if they know that there is someone who knows what they're doing and can answer questions and help troubleshoot their own issues. This is one reason why speakers begin with a short bio. They are explaining why you should trust what they say. This doesn't mean that the instructor has to be an industry expert, however. Students will often automatically assume that an instructor has more knowledge and experience than themselves and have enough subject authority to be able to teach them.

Feedback

The instructor can serve as a mirror to someone's progress and self-esteem during and after learning. Visual (eye contact and nods) and verbal ("good job" or "that's right") feedback to people's efforts, no matter how small, keep people connected and motivated. Some libraries even issue certificates at the end of programs and classes as proof of participation and accomplishment. Offering participants the chance to give feedback on the program, asking for suggestions as well as their impressions, makes people feel that their opinions can make a difference and are important.

Active Learning

All generations appreciate active learning, or the chance to practice the information and/or skills while they're still in the learning environment. This can include lecture-style situations as long as participants have the opportunity to ask questions. Active learning gives people the opportunity to prove to themselves that they understand material and can replicate results for themselves once they leave. In an online environment, at least for technology how-tos, the instructor can tell viewers to follow along or to pause the video and try it at home at certain intervals.

Highlight Relevancy

The previous chapters highlighted the importance of information relevance and applicability to adult learners. Make sure to engage your participants and ask questions. Why are they there? How are they going to use the information or skill? How will the information affect their lives? Even if they don't answer aloud, it will still make them mentally connect the lines between the class and their lives.

Taking It Home

Making instruction material available in person and online is important in order to reach all potential learners. In-person participants then have the instruction reiterated on the material for reference at home, which is a benefit when so many lament the modern lack of manuals and instructions. Class handouts and how-tos can be made available on library websites along with curated suggestions for online videos or even local classes. Even if the younger generations are the ones that claim a preference for self-study online, older generations with mobility or timing conflicts also then have access to the material.

Although generalizations may not always apply, an awareness of these generational commonalities can help libraries plan for and accommodate different learners. This doesn't only apply to serving the public. As public libraries regularly begin hiring shelvers in their early teens and retain employees well into (or past) their retirement years, these considerations also apply to library employee training and continuing education (Keegan 2011, 222–24). When these considerations are applied to the public, it can be especially helpful when libraries are trying to draw in specific age groups, such as Boomers or Millennials. It can be easy, through anecdotes, "popular knowledge," and even one's own experience, to apply these principles to individuals and groups out of hand. It is important that every librarian and instructor realize that these are generalizations and may not apply to every group or person.

BIBLIOGRAPHY

Ansoorian, Andrew, Pamela Good, and David Samuelson. 2003. "Managing Generational Differences." *Leadership* 32, no. 5 (May/June): 34–36.

Bart, Mary. 2011. "The Five R's of Engaging Millennial Students." *Teaching and Learning*, November 16, 2011. https://www.facultyfocus.com/articles/teaching-and-learning/the-five-rs-of-engaging-millennial-students/.

Coates, Julie. 2007. *Generational Learning Styles*. River Falls, WI: LERN Books.

Deal, J. J. 2007. *Retiring the Generation Gap: How Employees Young and Old Can Find Common Ground*. San Francisco: Jossey-Bass.

Dimock, Michael. 2019. "Defining Generations: Where Millennials End and Generation Z Begins." Pew Research Center, January 17, 2019. https://www.pewresearch.org/fact-tank/2019/01/17/where-millennials-end-and-generation-z-begins/.

Fry, Richard. 2018. "Millennials Are the Largest Generation in the Workforce." *Pew Research Center*, Washington, DC. http://www.pewresearch.org/fact-tank/2018/04/11/millennials-largest-generation-us-labor-force/ft_18-04-02_generationsdefined2017_working-age/.

Keegan, Kerry. 2011. "X, Y, and Z Are Call Numbers, Not Co-Workers: Communicating Through Generational Differences." *Feliciter* 57 (6): 222–24.

Loria, Kevin, and Samantha Lee. 2018. "Here's Which Generation You're Part of Based on Your Birth Year—and Why Those Distinctions Exist." *Business Insider*, April 19, 2018. https://www.businessin

sider.com/generation-you-are-in-by-birth-year-millennial-gen-x-baby-boomer-2018-3.

Martin, Jason. 2006. "I Have Shoes Older Than You: Generational Diversity in the Library." *The Southeastern Librarian* 54 (3): 4–11. https://digitalcommons.kennesaw.edu/seln/vol54/iss3/4.

Mohr, Kathleen A. J., and Eric S. Mohr. 2017. "Understanding Generation Z Students to Promote a Contemporary Learning Environment." *Journal on Empowering Teaching Excellence* 1 (1): 84–94.

Morris, Charles R. 1996. *The AAPR: America's Most Powerful Lobby and the Clash of Generations*. New York: Times Books.

Nikischer, Andrea. 2017. "Best Practices for Adult Educators Working in Cross-Generational Learning Spaces." *Adult Education Research Conference*. http://www.newprariepress.org/aerc/2017/papers/4.

Noel, Mary Alice, MD. 2016. "Do Millennials Need New Tactics for Teaching?" *The Uniformed Family Physician*, 31st ser., 10, no. 1 (Fall): 14–15. http://www.usafp.org/wp-content/uploads/2016/12/usafp37.pdf.

Pilcher, Jane. 1994. "Mannheim's Sociology of Generations: An Undervalued Legacy." *The British Journal of Sociology* 45 (3): 481–95. doi:10.2307/591659.

Prensky, Marc. 2001. "Digital Natives, Digital Immigrants Part 1." *On the Horizon—The Strategic Planning Resource for Educational Professionals* 9 (5): 1–6.

Social Security. n.d. "Benefits Planner: Retirement Social Security Administration." https://www.ssa.gov/planners/retire/applying2.html.

Zemke, Ron, Claire Raines, and Bob Filiczak. 1999. "Generation Gaps in the Classroom." *Training* 36 (11): 48–52, 54.

FIVE

Sensory Learning

A brief review of what we know about adult learners tells us that (1) they have a need or a problem to solve and (2) outside influences and experiences affect the way that they learn. A third consideration is that they have internal preferences, specifically sensory learning preferences, that can affect how people engage with information and even whether they remember it. This chapter examines the various ways that library staff can accommodate the learning style needs in a classroom, one-on-one, online, and through the phone.

Everyone has a favored way that they like to learn. Some prefer lectures, hands-on classes, or group discussions while others prefer to watch videos, learn online, read books, or just figure things out on their own. These various preferences are commonly divided into three categories, referred to as VAK: visual learners, auditory learners, and kinesthetic or mechanical learners (Gilakjani 2012, 105–6). The instructor has a preferred sensory method of teaching as well; one that usually reflects how they learn best. Knowing that other styles exists, what they are, and what that means for library instructions, can assist library staff to design learning opportunities that will help patrons connect with and retain information.

A QUICK LOOK AT HOW MEMORY WORKS

1. **Input**: Someone uses the senses to take in information.
2. **Working Memory**: If they are paying attention to the information, it goes into short-term, or working memory.

3. **Long-Term Memory**: If someone has the chance to use the information, apply it, or attach the information to something they already know, and then it has a better chance of staying in long-term memory. (McLeod 2012)

Sensory input is the first step to making sure that information makes it to working memory and tailoring it to their preferred learning "sense" can help people pay attention. There is no way to know a participants VAK style, but studies have shown that learning situations that contain elements from all three learning styles have a better chance at retention (Lemire 1998, 31–32). This is because most people are a mix of preferences and may not have a strong leaning toward one or the other. Others will have pronounced preferences that can make or break their ability to learn the material.

VISUAL LEARNERS

Visual learners are characterized by a preference for seeing a visual representation of information. This can refer to graphs, pictures, or even a sheet of instructions. All of this enhances their connection with the instructor and the information. Videos or even an animated presenter will keep them engaged and interested. They rely heavily on demonstration and being "walked through" a process. Visual learners will often want something to take home or something that they can connect to online to help them follow up on the information at home.

Common phrases from the group include "Can you do that again," "Let me watch you," or "I can't see what you did." Some instructors view these comments as an indication that someone wasn't paying attention, but their watching the process (sometimes multiple times) is cementing the information into their working memory.

HOW TO ACCOMMODATE VISUAL LEARNERS

In a Class

1. Incorporate pictures, graphics, videos or some form of multimedia into the presentation.
2. Have a handout with steps, pictures, or graphs.
3. Do physical demonstrations where everyone can see or have a video that shows the same process.

4. Have material they can take home or a list of links to highly visual websites, videos, or other instructional material.

5. Use animated gestures during class to keep them engaged.

One-on-One

When given a choice, visual learners will want a demonstration.

1. Have a handout, book, or other printed material for them to follow along or that backs up the demonstrated information.

2. If on a computer or device, demonstrate the process first and then ask them to reproduce the action. They may ask to see it done multiple times.

E-mail and Online

These two formats naturally lend themselves to visual learning, since it may be the only form of contact between the library and the patron. There may be many library products and services, databases and e-books, for example, which people may go immediately to the library site to access, only to find that they need help in its use. Pictures, GIFs, and even embedded videos along with step-by-step processes will help visual learners navigate and learn. E-mail templates should be made on commonly asked questions that contain the same information from the instructional page. Both should always be highly visual, since there is no way to tell whether the person on the other end is a visual learner.

On the Phone

The phone presents some potential roadblocks to visual learners, but most can be overcome by following along with the patron (when possible) on websites or through device processes. This will also help the library staff who are visually oriented to be able to help a patron "sight unseen." Many libraries have multiple devices, not for patron use, but for staff who need to work through such issues with patrons either in-house or over the phone.

AUDITORY LEARNERS

Auditory learners learn best through things being explained verbally and aloud. Lectures, discussions, audiobooks, and even the audio portion of videos are helpful to this group. They also may find it beneficial to voice their process out loud, either to themselves, fellow students, or to their instructor. "Talking through it" is their way of paying attention to the information: organizing it against preexisting information in order to move it to short- and then long-term memory. Being able to ask questions and flush out ideas and understanding is paramount to understanding. This is why, even if they can learn from passively listening (say, from an audiobook) engaging verbally with an instructor works even better.

HOW TO ACCOMMODATE AUDITORY LEARNERS

In a Class

1. Explain steps and process out loud.
2. Paraphrase content on a screen. This avoids the annoying practice of reading directly off of a screen, but still makes the content available to audio learners.
3. Allow time for questions and anecdotes. Give clear instructions as to when they can ask (anytime versus at the end) to avoid interruptions or frustration.
4. Offer suggestions for video or audiobooks for further information on the topic.

One-on-One

When given a choice, auditory learners will want you to explain before or during a demonstration.

1. Explain steps and the process as they are being demonstrated.
2. Have them talk through the process as they practice.
3. Encourage them to ask questions or share experiences about their question or the process.

E-mail and Online

Highly auditory-based learners may actually avoid modes of contact that don't allow for a back and forth conversation. If they do, their e-mails may be highly detailed and verbose to make up for the lack. The response, as mentioned with visual learners, should contain multiple styles, which for an audio learner means incorporating media if it is available. If possible, instructional pages on the library website should have video tutorials of common library tasks and products.

On the Phone

A predominantly auditory learner will probably call the library with a question or for help (rather than e-mail) if given the chance. They will not want to be directed to a website or sent instructions via e-mail. Instead, they want to be walked through the process verbally. They may also call and outline a process to *you*, just make sure to themselves that they have it right before they try to perform it.

KINESTHETIC/MECHANICAL LEARNERS

Kinesthetic learners learn best by physically interacting in some way with the material. Device or software classes, or any class where someone can follow along by mimicking the information or process will work best to engage this group with the material. "Let me try it" is one of the most common phrases that indicate a strong mechanical inclination. Writing notes or drawing processes during visual or auditory instruction is a way for them to "mechanize" the process and move the information into working memory. This may be true even if outlines or handouts are already provided.

HOW TO ACCOMMODATE KINESTHETIC LEARNERS
In the Class

1. Have tables, paper, and writing utensils available for those who want to take notes (especially in a lecture format).
2. Either provide computers or encourage people to bring their own devices for software, device, or website classes so that they follow along.

3. Show participants how to pause videos and minimize an application so that they practice at home.

One-on-One

1. Use a computer or device on which they can perform the steps and processes. Let them do everything and just talk them through it. Avoid the inclination to do it for them.
2. Offer pencil and paper so that they can write instructions or notes.
3. Demonstrate how to pause videos and minimize an application so that they practice at home.

E-mail and Online

Kinesthetic learners are generally game to follow instructions, since they want to try it themselves, anyway. Language and steps that clearly detail processes, encourage people, and stress a positive outcome should be used in both formats.

On the Phone

A kinesthetic learner will often fare well over the phone because they necessarily have to either act out instructions as they're being told them or they are taking notes. "Say that again. I'm writing this down" is something many library staff have encountered in phone conversations with this group.

A fourth variation, reading/writing, was suggested as an addition to the sensory model in the 1990s (Zubair Baig and Mahmood Ahmad 2016, 6698; Fleming and Mills 1992, 137). This model suggests that there are some learners who prefer information specifically in its written form. They would rather read instructions, whether it be on a PowerPoint, an instruction sheet, or in a book. Reading/writing dominant learners are less likely to seek another person to help them learn, but they will use the library as a resource for books, brochures, handouts, and other forms of written information and instruction.

PULLING IT TOGETHER: MULTIMODAL TEACHING

It is worth restating: library staff are not going to know the sensory learning style of every person that comes to class, comes to the desk, or contacts the library for help. And despite personal preference, most people are a mix of the different learning styles, or multimodal in how they learn (Shams and Seitz 2008, 411–15). In order to accommodate the most types (which is the ideal so that the instructor doesn't have to redo his or her teaching design for every class), it important to incorporate multiple aspects of the sensory styles into all possible instructional settings.

Common Phrases	**Sensory Learning Type**
Show me . . .	Visual
Tell me . . .	Auditory
Let me try . . .	Kinesthetic
Can you say it again?	Auditory
Do you have instructions?	Visual
Is this available online?	Visual/Auditory

WAYS TO ACCOMMODATE ALL SENSORY LEARNERS

In a Class or Program

1. Have tables and writing material for those who want to take notes (kinesthetic).
2. Have presentation material in the form of an overhead projection or physical materials (visual).
3. Have handouts and written recommendations for online and print resources (visual).
4. Have an engaging speaker (visual and audio).
5. Build in time for questions, anecdotes, and discussion (audio).
6. Have computers or devices to follow along and practice when applicable (visual and kinesthetic).

One-on-One

This situation actually allows library staff to *ask* the patron how they would like to taught. "Do you want me show you or would you like me to talk you through it?" "Would you like to take notes or I have an instruction sheet you can take home?" These are simple questions and suggestions whose answers are a direct indication of someone's learning style. People who have multiple sensory styles may request more than one way of interaction ("I'm going to watch you and take notes and then I'll try it"). Anyone instructing one-on-one has to be especially careful to not teach toward their own style with the well-meaning thought that "this is how I would want to be taught." Teaching specifically in another style other than your own can feel uncomfortable at first, but with practice and reflection on how much it benefits the other party, it will get easier and more enjoyable.

E-mail and Online

These formats are the most important in which to incorporate all sensory styles (if possible) because there is little to no opportunity to gauge the other party's style and respond accordingly. Online instructional material, especially, tends to be static and is not frequently changed. Making sure that there are clear instructions and visuals, links to further resources or videos, and contact information on how to get more help are a good way to make sure that all styles are being accommodated.

On the Phone

Like the one-on-one, phone calls offer the chance to ask the patron how they want the information. Sometimes they do not know that information is available online or that libraries can send links and instructions through e-mail. Depending on the interaction, library staff could then either talk them through their need or offer the information in a form more palatable to their preferred style.

If it's important to consider what sensory accommodations libraries can make for patrons, it is equally important to pay attention to the needs of the library staff. Besides in-house training and personal research, there are many continuing education opportunities available through state associations, private vendors, and national associations such as ALA. Conferences, in-person training, and even live webinars can accommodate most, if not all learning styles. Possessing an awareness of your own learning style can help you pick and choose the continuing education and training that will do you the most good. If you are a presenter for such events, this information will not only benefit your library patrons, but those to whom you teach in and for the field.

BIBLIOGRAPHY

Fleming, Neil D., and Colleen Mills. 1992. "Not Another Inventory, Rather a Catalyst for Reflection." *To Improve the Academy* 11: 137.

Gilakjani, Abbas Pourhossein. 2012. "Visual, Auditory, Kinaesthetic Learning Styles and Their Impact on English Language Teaching." *Journal of Studies in Education* 2 (1): 104–13.

Khalil, Mohammed K., and Ihsan A. Elkhider. 2016. "Applying Learning Theories and Instructional Design Models for Effective Instruction." *Advances in Physiological Education* 40 (2): 147–56.

Lemire, David. 1998. "Three Learning Styles Models: Research and Recommendations for Developmental Education." *The Learning Assistance Review* (Fall): 26–40.

McLeod, S. A. 2012. "Working Memory." *Simply Psychology*. https://www.simplypsychology.org/working%20memory.html.

Merrill, M. David. 2001. "First Principles of Instruction." *Journal of Structural Learning & Intelligent Systems* 14 (4): 459. https://sso.kent.edu/cas/login.

Shams, Ladan, and Aaron R. Seitz. 2008. "Benefits of Multisensory Learning." *Trends in Cognitive Science* 12 (11): 411–17. http://faculty.ucr.edu/~aseitz/pubs/Shams_Seitz08.pdf.

Zubair Baig, Mirza, and Mudassar Mahmood Ahmad. 2016. "Learning with a Style: The Role of Learning Styles and Models in Academic Success." *European Academic Research* 4 (8): 6695–705.

SIX

Cultural Considerations of
Library Instruction

The United States is world-renowned for its cultural mix of humanity. Culture encompasses a variety of elements, a few of which include race, ethnicity, religion, gender identity, geographic region, sexual orientation, and socioeconomic status. Whether conscious or not, culture acts like a lens through which information and interactions are processed. All students and teachers bring their culture with them to every instructional interaction. Library staff, as well as library organizations, who are culturally empathetic and realize the potential impact of culture on instruction have a better chance at offering a transformational learning experience. This library service can then foster a beneficial and lasting relationship between, not only individuals but also entire communities.

CULTURE AND THE TEACHER

The terms "culture," "cultural intelligence," and "cultural competence" have gained significant importance as communities become more diverse. One definition of culture is, "the shared, yet unarticulated assumptions that permeate thought and action" (Merriam and Bierema 2014, 240). This shows that culture and thinking are inseparable and that someone may not even be aware of the influence of their own cultural bias until it contrasts against another. Library instructors may notice someone not interacting with the class or the information in the same way as others, or that the same one-on-one session that has worked countless times is not working in that instructional instance. There is always the possibility that cultural influences are the reason for the disparity.

Cultural intelligence and competence can help library staff overcome potential cultural barriers in all interactions, not just in instruction. Both terms have to do with an individual's ability to interact with, understand, appreciate, and accommodate those with a different culture (Ang, Van Dyne, and Koh 2006, 100–23). Cultural intelligence is specific to someone's ability to adapt to various cultural situations successfully. Cultural competence is a broader concept and process that includes becoming familiar with one's own cultural influences while learning about and appreciating other cultures (Griffer and Perlis 2007, 30). This is a personal, conscious, and purposeful process that is location-specific depending on the library service area, since populations can change from branch to branch as well as from city to county.

There are a variety of ways to build cultural intelligence and competence. Becoming skilled and comfortable at addressing the needs of various cultures starts first with a general appreciation of diversity. That includes a personal awareness of one's own culture and how it plays a role in everyday perceptions and interactions. This contributes to empathy and an awareness of others. The purposeful interaction with individuals or groups from another culture produces cultural appreciation and contextual understanding. This is a potentially a lifelong process, as no one can know everything about every culture, and populations in a given service area can change over time. These practical efforts toward understanding will be reflected in all interactions but especially during instructional instances where trust and comfort are integral to learning.

Steps to Gain Cultural Competence and Intelligence

1. Cultivate an appreciation for diversity.
2. Have self-awareness about your own cultural identity.
3. Purposefully interact with others from different cultures.

Equity, diversity, and inclusion are listed as some of the ALA's key action areas and apply to a variety of library aspects such as programming, outreach, library workforce, and education (ALA 2008). The ALA stresses the importance of having representative staff and community advocates on library staff whenever possible and has even created resources and strategies to help libraries develop a diverse workforce (ALA 2011). Having cultural representatives on the board or in other influential roles, such as panels, can help a library stay connected to the needs and interests of diverse populations. Language differences will always be a potential barrier to access, so encouraging multilingual staff, offering translation services, offering material in local languages, and making library website and catalog translation available prove an awareness and willingness to connect and serve. Outreach services and programs to communities and neighborhoods are also an important tool for libraries and help resolve misconceptions and issues of access.

CULTURE AND THE STUDENT

Someone's culture can have a direct influence on the way they use or perceive a public library. One potential difference is the fact that not all public libraries work the same way around the world, if they exist at all in the person's country of origin. Librarians may also not play the same inter-active, instructive role. Some libraries are membership institutions where users pay a fee for access to materials and services. Others are mainly seen as the province of students. Some services, such as free Internet use, free circulation of materials, reference help, or technology and class offer-ings may not be commonly offered. Other institutions may be closely tied to authority or government entities and be seen as a potential way to track or monitor those who use it and are therefore to be avoided. These differ-ences of perception, purpose, and access are one of the first things that U.S. libraries may have to address with new immigrant populations in order to get them through the doors.

The roles of student and teacher as well as the very definition of knowl-edge may be different from culture to culture. Western societies generally view the acquisition of knowledge as an individual endeavor in that the learner is responsible for getting and retaining it. Even its possible applica-tions are often thought of as applying only to the individual. In contrast, some Eastern cultures see learning as a communal responsibility because what people learn will affect their thoughts and actions and have a trickle-down effect on the entire community (Ishimura and Bartlett 2014, 313–26). Some view personal study as the norm and class as the place where the pieces get put together to form an understandable picture; whereas, for others, class is where they get all of their information. The role of the teacher can be different from culture to culture as well, with some being an authoritarian, fact-giving figure who should not be questioned out of respect, or a parental-like figure who is meant to be a sounding board for new information and ideas. The implied effectiveness and capabilities of an instructor may also vary depending on what that culture values. Someone may be judged solely on credentials (has three degrees and is a manager) or there may be more value in experience (has taught the subject for twenty years).

The behavior of a student in any instructional setting may be a direct result of culture. Verbal and nonverbal traits that some attribute to shyness, outspokenness, boredom, a lack of understanding, disrespect, or feelings about the class and the instructor may all be normal from someone else's perspective. Time considerations, such as the notion of tardiness or promptness, can differ greatly around the world and can be seen as a matter of personal respect. Issues of personal space, the level of discussion and class involvement, and how students and teachers show interest and respect are all common divergences in culture, even within U.S. culture.

BEST PRACTICES IN MULTICULTURAL INSTRUCTION

Everyone wants empathy, respect, understanding, patience, and a non-judgmental setting in which to learn. This starts with the instructor and the library organization purposefully seeking to attain cultural intelligence and competency regarding their specific service population. A familiarization with the community's cultural make up and their specific needs and interests will result in responsive and useful classes, programming, staffing decisions, and resources and help to overcome potential barriers to access and understanding.

Library staff play an important part in making sure that patrons feel physically and mentally safe, especially in an instructional setting. Purposefully stating the role and responsibilities of the instructor can help those unfamiliar with the setting to understand how to act and interact with the instructor as well as other students. Instructions on how to ask questions, such as "let me know if you need me to repeat it," "raise your hand," or "we'll take questions at the end," or a quick outline of how the class is organized, such as "I'll talk about the subject and then we'll practice," give people a framework in which to organize their thoughts and participate. The physical setting of a classroom, lecture, or a one-on-one regarding the closeness of other participants or even how close you are supposed to be to the instructor may all be a matter of cultural expectation and comfort. Having more seating than is technically needed can help ameliorate potential issues and give people the space they need to feel comfortable (and pay attention).

The instructor is responsible for making sure that the library environment remains welcoming and conducive to learning for all. A perceived negative reaction from other patrons to culturally different participants' appearance or culture would be detrimental not only to their feelings of safety and welcome but also would affect their ability to learn and their desire to attend other functions, seek instruction, and even frequent the library for any reason. Libraries should have clear behavioral policy statements on the expectations of staff and other patrons as well as training on how to handle such situations. If these are not addressed before something occurs, there may be personal and organizational repercussions that can affect public perception of the library as well as community relationships. There is also safety and comfort for staff in having clear guidelines and the backing of the library to address threats to address inappropriate behavior.

Multimodal teaching, or varying the way information is presented, has been proven effective as a learning tool for multicultural settings (Foster 2018, 585). It is important to make sure that verbal and written instructions use clear, jargon-free language in order to reach the widest possible audience and avoid potential language barriers. If a service area has a large population of non-English speakers, there may be local interest groups or associations that are willing to assist with document translation or even classes in their native language using library resources. Recorded classes should include captioning, a function that is automatically included in many video creation software. Translation services can also be used to translate scripts and captions, so that any recorded classes or demonstrations are then accessible to those who do not feel comfortable or have the skill set to attend a class given in English. Including images from that culture in marketing material, presentations, and instructional material, whether people or ideological pictures, will show that their culture is included in the library's organizational and community culture.

U.S. libraries serve an important function in that, as the ALA states, "an informed public constitutes the very foundation of a democracy" (ALA 2012). As libraries and their staff seek to accommodate and appreciate diversity, they are also imparting and educating others in an important aspect of U.S. culture: the right to learn and better yourself through your own efforts. As Patrick Parrish and Jennifer Linder-VanBerschot write, "fundamentally, when we teach, we are teaching culture" (2010, 5). Not every aspect of culture is going to affect an instructional setting, but basic interaction and a shared purpose can garner acceptance, understanding, and even comradery between participants.

BIBLIOGRAPHY

American Library Association. 2008. "Equity, Diversity, and Inclusion." http://www.ala.org/advocacy/diversity.

American Library Association. 2011. "Recruiting for Diversity." http://www.ala.org/advocacy/diversity/workforcedevelopmentfordiversity.

American Library Association. 2012. "Democracy Statement." http://www.ala.org/aboutala/governance/officers/past/kranich/demo/statement.

Ang, Soon, Linn Van Dyne, and Christine Koh. 2006. "Personality Correlates of the Four-Factor Model of Cultural Intelligence." *Group & Organization Management* 31 (1): 100–123. doi:10.1177/1059601105275267.

Foster, Elizabeth. 2018. "Cultural Competence in Library Instruction: A Reflective Practice Approach." *Libraries and the Academy* 18 (3): 575–93.

Griffer, Mona R., and Susan M. Perlis. 2007. "Developing Cultural Intelligence in Preservice Speech-Language Pathologists and Educators." *Communication Disorders Quarterly* 29 (1): 28–35. https://doi.org/10.1177/1525740107312546.

Ishimura, Yusuke, and Joan C. Bartlett. 2014. "Are Librarians Equipped to Teach International Students? A Survey of Current Practices and Recommendations for Training." *Journal of Academic Librarianship* 40: 313–21.

Merriam, Sharan B., and Laura L. Bierema. 2014. *Adult Learning: Linking Theory and Practice*. San Francisco: Jossey-Bass.

Parrish, Patrick, and Jennifer A. Linder-VanBerschot. 2010. "Cultural Dimensions of Learning: Addressing the Challenges of Multicultural Instruction." *International Review of Research in Open & Distance Learning* 11 (2): 1–19.

SEVEN

Passive Instruction

Not every moment of instruction is done from person to person. For some, speaking to staff will always be a last resort when they need help. Others are simply unaware of the tools available to them. They aren't avoiding knowledge or instruction; they simply don't know it's an option. Passive instruction in this chapter refers to situations where individuals are able to access learning material without the aid of another person for the express intention of self-instruction. This way of offering instruction is especially valuable in any situation where manpower and staff time are an issue such as in small libraries or where there are budget constraints for programming and classes. Quality material in any medium means that people of all ages and learning types can benefit from library-facilitated instruction.

Passive materials can be books, media, links, displays, videos, instructions, libguides, and class handouts. Class or program handouts are included in this definition because they are meant to go with the participants to help them retain information and potentially practice new skills. Handouts also serve as an aid to self-directed learners who want the class's content but are unable to attend. Instruction sheets for common tasks and procedures, such as how to download library e-books or how to renew material, educate patrons in modern library functions and services. Floor displays of books and media highlight much-needed instructional material and put it directly in the path of those who might need it. The creation and placement of database guides, or libguides, connect users to valuable (and expensive) databases. The library website and catalog can bring this same information to patrons, along with the added possibility of video tutorials or instructive GIFs. This material can be created and utilized by staff for a variety of active instructional encounters, but they are also invaluable learning tools for all of those who will come across them on their own at the library, at outreach locations, or online.

Passive material has the potential to reach a larger audience than a single staff member could hope to encounter. Instead of relying solely on the foot-traffic paths in the physical library, libraries can place a variety of passive material in popular community locations, senior centers, hospital waiting rooms, bus stops, or malls. Some libraries have created partnerships with local tablet and e-book reader vendors where these instructions, highlighting free material for an expensive product, are displayed along with the product. Hospitals, doctor's offices, and workout facilities can display library resources on consumer health and wellness as well as a calendar of upcoming library programs. Besides providing useful information where people live their daily lives, these off-site locations provide continual and visible proof that the library is still pertinent and that its resources and services are still of value to the community.

INSTRUCTIONAL DESIGN

Instructional design, or the "creation of learning experiences and materials in a manner that results in the acquisition and application of knowledge and skills," is quickly becoming a core component to many ALA-accredited library science programs as more and more of the profession engages in public instruction (ATD 2018). This systematic approach can assist in not only the creation of classes and programs but also in any instructional print or media creation. A popular instructional design method in library applications is known as ADDIE (see Figure 7.1), which stands for analyze, design, develop, implement, and evaluate (Turner 2016, 477–78). The chart below demonstrates how ADDIE could be used in the creation of an instruction sheet for how to download e-books.

ADDIE Process
Project: "How to download an e-book" instruction sheet

Analyze   The audience is iPhone, Android, and Kindle users. The goal is for them to access e-Media on devices using either the app or the website to get Kindle books. The objective is that staff can use it to teach patrons about e-books and passive users will be able to use the instructions and set up their device or access e-books without staff.

Device-type-specific or one for apps, Kindles, and web? Who will be the audience? What questions will the instructions answer? What are potential barriers that can't be addressed on a guide? Will the guide be device-specific or broad? Where will they be displayed?

Design   The guide is for class and passive use.
Choose the screenshots.
Meant for Android and Apple users one side and Kindle instructions on the other.
Make sure there are elements for various learning types.
Consider a layout for a large print version of paper material.

Develop   Create and assemble content.

Implement   Test the instructions for clarity and usability and any web content or media for accessibility. Train staff in its content and use with patrons.

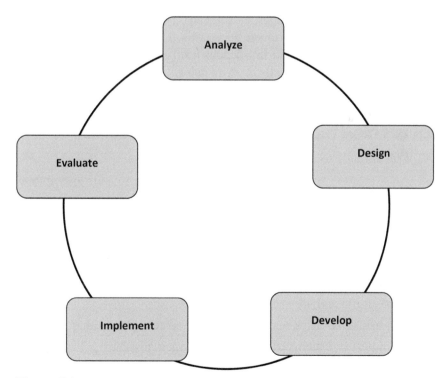

Figure 7.1. ADDIE Instruction Design Method

Evaluate Gather feedback throughout the process. Assess the movement of material from passive displays and its effectiveness in classes. Gather staff feedback on its use with patrons. Follow up with patrons. Track hits or downloads on the website if applicable.

The evaluation stage, despite being listed at the end, should happen throughout the entire process. Apps, software, and technology in general change constantly, so a careful review of instructional material should routinely be made to make sure that it is current. Whatever the application, this system can aid in the creation of instructional content.

WRITING AND ILLUSTRATIONS

Language and illustrations are essential considerations in any library material to aid in understanding and access. Besides spelling and grammar, content creators need to keep in mind issues such as readability, clarity, and reading level. The U.S. government considered the readability and accessibility of information such an important issue that they passed the Plain Writing Act of 2010 to apply to government documents. This set of guidelines details how to write information and instructions for the largest possible audience. Although the Act doesn't legally apply to public libraries, the guidelines and principles can serve as a useful tool when creating instructional content.

TEN TIPS FROM THE FEDERAL PLAIN LANGUAGE GUIDELINES

1. Write directly to the reader (you and you're).
2. Use a question and answer format where possible to address common questions and avoid ambiguity.
3. Use common, single or double-syllable words.
4. Use consistent wording throughout the document.
5. Use the active tense instead of the passive tense.
6. Use declarative with few adjectives or adverbs.
7. Avoid jargon and use short, simple sentences.
8. Use positive phrasing and avoid negative words (don't, can't).
9. Use bullets or lists instead of sentences when possible.
10. Highlight important steps or concepts using bold and italics. (GSE 2011, 1–118)

Whether writing for paper, webpages, or scripting media such as videos, the application of these guidelines in library material help keep all content accessible to the widest possible audience.

Large Print

Font size is another important consideration considering that as of 2015 three out of every four Americans need some form of vision correction (Kooley 2015). According to the American Foundation for the Blind, large print starts at font size eighteen (Duffey, n.d.). Normally associated with books and senior populations, there are people of every age and situation that benefit from large print, library-created materials and instructions. Time, effort, and cost are all factors when producing (or reproducing) library documents in large print. A size-twelve-font document that is changed to large print considerably changes the page count and graphics placement in print and online materials and for that reason may significantly increase reproduction cost. These materials, or at least a webpage with the same information, can be made available on the library website for instant access for patrons and library staff. Even if every class handout or guide on display isn't in large print, libraries should consider at least creating large print versions, graphics included, that can be printed on demand for those who need or prefer the accommodation.

Illustrations and Lists

Concise, visually accessible information can draw the eye to important information and provide clarity. The adage of a picture being worth a thousand words is especially true for visual learners and may be essential for trying to describe certain topics or processes. Copyright and reproduction rights apply to all print and web applications, so gain permission where needed and properly caption, label, and accredit reproductions in all material. Bullet pointed or numbered lists, circles, and other directional guides visually separate information, and highlight key points.

Titles and Headers

The title and headers will naturally draw passive learners if they are engaging and speak to the resolution of a specific need. Those who access the material outside of a class or program setting should be able to access the same key points and processes as those who attend.

Titles That Get to the Point

- 10 Tips for Interviews
- Microsoft Word Basics: 5 Essential Functions
- How the 1918 Flu Changed the World
- How to Download an e-book: For Smartphones and Tablets

PRESENTING INFORMATION

The presentation of passive instruction can happen in many forms, some of which include class handouts, program guides, libguides, instruction sheets, bookmarks, and displays. These can be a single or multipage document and, as mentioned previously, are meant to convey the key points of a topic and illustrate and explain processes. Each of these forms has strengths and weaknesses depending on its construction and application in passive instruction. Beyond content and writing style, the document should accommodate as many learning types as possible and address the pertinent needs of both the patron and the library.

To avoid reinventing the wheel, libraries can also seek permission from other libraries to use or recreate their handouts and other instructional material. Some sites already exist for this purpose, such as the Ohio Library Council's *Helping Each Other Out* webpage, run by the Reference and Information Services Division. Libraries upload their handouts, instructions, guides, and even PowerPoint presentations with the express permission for others to use and modify the content. A simple web search will bring up a variety of library-made guides and other creations that can be used by other libraries or for inspiration and ideas.

Class Handouts

There will be differences in the information layout depending on the style and topic. An example would be how the handout of a history lecture on wartime medical advances would be very different from a class on how to use Excel. The first may contain a list of medical innovations or pictures of gadgets while the second might highlight common workflows and processes of Excel. If a PowerPoint is used in class, the instructor may be tempted to use the "handout" feature to produce a reproduction of slides with note-taking capabilities as the class handout. This decision should be made based from the legibility of texts and pictures when scaled down to the needed degree.

Bookmarks and Libguides

Bookmarks are a quick way to highlight a useful resource or to describe short processes. These are ideal for displays, placing inside related material, or for placing at outreach locations. Database vendors, such as EBSCOhost or Overdrive, will often provide materials to libraries in order to promote their resources.

Libguides are materials that specifically provide information and instruction on library resources and databases. They should reflect the language of the online library portal to the same information and quickly state the purpose of the resource in such a way as to call to potential users. Like bookmarks, many vendors will have online resource kits that can be locally branded and include media, printable instructions, as well as embeddable video tutorials or GIFs for library websites. At the very least, they serve as examples for libraries that want to create their own material from scratch.

Displays

One of the most prolific barriers to information and instruction is the ignorance that it exists. Signage and displays, where material and information are put directly in the path of potential learners, are one of the oldest forms of passive instruction in libraries. Where they are placed is of paramount importance to the successful access of instructional material in the physical library and at outreach locations. Signage and material should be highly visible and accessible without staff assistance. A central location for such material is also advisable, as studies have shown that someone will remember where they found helpful material and associate the location with other helpful material (Butler 2008, 100–101). Such material should also be placed in appropriate topic-specific areas, such as a language database guide in the English speakers of other languages (ESOL) or foreign language book section or a class guide from a scholarship how-to class by the college finance material. Varying the ways and means of access increase not only use but also awareness, which is useful since an adult learner may not try to access the information until they have a need in the future.

Instructive books, audiobooks, and videos often comprise large and popular collections that can make for useful and popular displays. This material should be circulatable, current (information-wise), and be in good condition. Related library ephemera that highlight library classes, recommended reading lists, or applicable online resources can be displayed along with these collections.

Library Website and Catalog

The library website has the greatest potential audience, with its 24/7 and "worldwide" passive access. Tutorials, downloadable handouts, videos, and GIFs on the library website and social media sites make learning material available at any time to anyone. A landing page that makes known all available materials introduces browsers or one-time shoppers to other content (see Figure 7.1). Applicable material can be linked on class and program event pages as a means of previewing and accessing class material. Tag these materials and even catalog them so that the content is searchable by the library catalog, linking a user not just with books and media but also streaming or downloadable content and applicable databases.

CONSIDERING THE COSTS

Reproduction costs may prevent budget-conscious libraries from placing materials in high-traffic areas or reproducing them outside of a program. Depending on the content, there may also be a cost to reproduce images in addition to the printing costs. Some libraries print on demand, relying on signage to direct patrons to staff or to a desk. Making materials available online or as downloadable content is a viable option for both staff and patron access.

Many libraries do not have their own marketing department to help with branding, layout, and images, and all material is instead produced by librarians or other staff. Documents can be created with a variety of products, including standard office software, online programs, or production tools that require a separate purchase. Five common production tools that can be used to create documents that contain logos, pictures, and text are:

- Adobe InDesign
- Canva (free online): https://www.canva.com

- Scribus (free online): https://www.scribus.net
- Inkscape (free online): https://inkscape.org
- Microsoft Publisher (Microsoft Office Suite)

These tools all contain templates and graphics that can aid the novice or the expert in creating quality material. Tutorials for these exist on the websites as well as on video tutorial sites such as YouTube, Lynda.com, and others that are a quick web search away.

BIBLIOGRAPHY

American Foundation for the Blind (AFB). 2018. "Facts and Figures on Adults with Vision Loss." *Blindness and Statistics*. http://www.afb.org/info/blindness-statistics/adults/facts-and-figures/2.

Association for Talent Development (ATD). 2018. "What Is Instructional Design?" *Talent Development Glossary Terms*. https://www.td.org/what-is-instructional-design.

Butler, Walter. 2008. "Re-Establishing Memory: Memory's Functions and the Reference Librarian." *Reference Services Review* 36 (1): 97–110. https://doi.org/10.1108/00907320810852069.

Duffy, Maureen A. n.d. "Using Large Print." *Essential Skills: Reading, Writing, and Vision Loss*. http://www.visionaware.org/info/every day-living/essential-skills/reading-writing-and-vision-loss/large-print/1234.

General Service Administration (GSE). 2011. *Federal Plain Language Guidelines*. 1–118. https://www.plainlanguage.gov/media/Federal-PLGuidelines.pdf.

Kooley, Steve. 2015. "US Optical Overview and Outlook." *Digital Eye Strain | The Vision Council*, December. https://www.thevision council.org/sites/default/files/Q415-Topline-Overview-Presenta tion-Stats-with-Notes-FINAL.PDF.

NoveList. 2014. "NoveList Plus Bookmarks." *Novelist Promotion Kit*. http://support.ebsco.com/promotion/promo_resources/Files/Col3/Nove List/NoveList Plus/NoveList_Plus_Bookmark_Printable2014.pdf.

Reference and Information Services Division. n.d. "Helping Each Other Out: Class Handouts and Downloads." *OLC-RISD*. https://olcrisd.word press.com/helping-each-other-out-class-handouts-and-downloads/.

Turner, Jennifer. 2016. "Instructional Design: Skills to Benefit the Library Profession." *Libraries and the Academy* 16 (3): 477–89.

EIGHT

Helping the Individual

Teaching One-on-One

Whether it's teaching a new user how to use the catalog, showing someone how to use a database for a research project, or how to attach a resume to an e-mail, one-on-one teaching is the most likely scenario for the majority of public librarians who work with adults. These encounters are different from a group setting in a number of ways, not just because of the number of people involved but also because the patron is usually the one to initiate the session. Individual instruction can almost always be considered part of a reference interview. A skillful reference interview, active listening skills, and a basic understanding of adult learners can result in productive and enjoyable instructional sessions that increase the value of the library to individuals and the community (Rader 1980, 97–98).

TIME, PLACE, AND OPPORTUNITY

Not every reference transaction or patron interaction results in a teachable moment. Those who do could happen across a variety of formats including face-to-face, over the telephone, or virtually using chats and e-mail. Telephone and virtual interactions are always patron-initiated, while in the physical library the staff may be the ones to engage the potential learner. There are three different ways that a librarian can interact with an in-house patron about their instructional needs. The first is when, like a phone call or e-mail, the patron is the one to specifically ask for instruction, such as "Can someone show me how to do this?" Help in trouble shooting accounts, online catalogs, and other library resources are common reasons for patrons to contact the library and are often referred to as bibliographic instruction. Even one instance of teaching patrons how to use a library resource can instill the awareness and value of information literacy, causing them to either seek more on their own or to ask for help sooner the next time they need help (Hays 2014, 4). The abundance of technology and software classes offered by libraries has taught the public that they can get assistance with non-library-related questions as well.

The second type of instructional interaction occurs when a patron asks for a resource or information and the staff recognizes that there is a resource that could address their need. The prevalence of both library and online resources means that there is a high chance staff may be directing the patron to an electronic resource. Even if the answer to their question lies in a paper resource, there is usually a learning curve or a process of navigation needed in order to access the needed information. The process of learning how to use a seemingly complicated resource may not seem worth it on their own, if they were even aware of it, but a short instructional encounter that produces the needed information in a few steps helps prove that it is worth the effort. Smartphones, tablets, and e-book capabilities are a good example of connecting users with unfamiliar resources. Patrons may often mistake an e-book in the catalog for a physical one. When they seek assistance in "finding" the book, staff have the opportunity to tell them what an e-book is and to show them how to get it on their device. It is often an "easy sell" because the patron wants the book, it may be the only one there, and they already have the means to get it. This is true for most adult's information needs in that there is usually some resource or tool that would benefit them. The librarian has the unique privilege of connecting patrons to resources, something that might not have happened if the librarian had not initially offered to teach them how.

The third encounter is entirely up to the librarian and involves approaching patrons who have not asked for either information or instruction. This decision would be based on what section they were in, what material they were carrying, or an observation of what they were searching or working on. A tactful approach is required because they may have specific reasons for not contacting staff such as time constraints, a belief in their own abilities and knowledge of resources, or an active avoidance of other people. A simple statement, though, can speak to an adult learner's problem-solving need or wish for expediency: "Can I show you something that can help you?" Showing someone in the car repair section how to search YouTube to find multiple solutions to his particular car problem is one example of connecting a user with a potentially unknown resource. Another might be overhearing someone say that they wish there was a way to see a list of books they had gotten from the library in the past and then showing them the "reading history" function on their account. It takes a service-oriented mentality to go strictly beyond what is being asked and seek opportunities to provide assistance, but the rewards are often that patrons learn that staff are a useful and friendly resource.

INSTRUCTION AND THE REFERENCE INTERVIEW

There are basic knowledge and skills that are critical to anyone being a good library instructor. First, there must be an interest and a will to provide good service. This means that the staff member with the most knowledge and skill in any given technology or resource may not be the best teacher for that subject if he or she doesn't have an actual desire to help someone learn. The genuine desire to help people teaches and instills patience and can be a driving force behind acquiring teaching skills and building relationships. The second aspect of being a good teacher is knowledge of available resources and having the skills required for a particular position, since not every job in the library has the same duties or expectations. A familiarity with the various factors that might affect adult learners provides insight into how individual instruction might be modified from person to person to best suit their learning preference. That way they have a greater chance of retaining information. Actively using this information can create a unique and beneficial experience for each patron. Each successful encounter also provides valuable feedback to the instructor, allowing him or her to learn from experience and grow in ability.

The first hurdle in even a potential teaching transaction is getting people to talk to staff. The Reference and User Services Association (RUSA), a division of the ALA, has identified five factors in the reference interview, specifically in the behavior of the librarian, that contribute to a positive experience (see Figure 8.1). These apply to all forms of contact, whether in person, by telephone, or virtually.

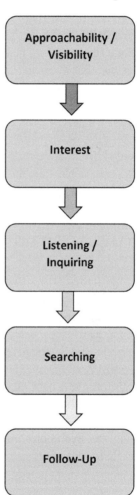

Figure 8.1. RUSA Behavioral Guidelines for Reference (RUSA 2016).

Approachability

The first guideline refers to the approachability or visibility of the librarian or staff. This is often the determining factor of whether someone chooses to interact with staff and get help or whether they try everything on their own. Some people are shy, nervous about interrupting staff while they appear to be busy, or simply unfamiliar with how to interact with staff and will wait for a verbal or nonverbal sign before they try to engage with staff. Are there signs directing people to help, nametags, or other identifiable features that denote that someone is a staff member? The fact that a library offers instruction, device help, or other personal tutorials is a service that many in the public are unaware of. Eye contact and a welcoming manner that includes a smile, as well as setting aside other activities and conversations, are cues that a patron is welcome. Acknowledging those who are waiting, even if it's just with eye contact and smile or nod, is a promise of help and can encourage patience. Visibility in a phone or virtual setting means that the contact information is highly visible and readily accessible on the library website. This means that the contact information language is easily identifiable in terms such as "Ask a Question" or "Contact Us" and is placed in site locations normally associated with help information such as headers, footers, sidebars, and menus (U.S. Department of Health and Human Services 2006, 90–91).

Interest

The second factor is exhibiting interest in the person and their issue. Some patrons are wary of instructional scenarios because they might have experienced a negative or judgmental reaction from family, friends, or workmates because they didn't know how to do something. They may be self-conscious over their lack of skills and feel like "everyone" else already knows all about the subject. Some simply do not like to admit "ignorance" of a subject or skill. A positive tone of voice, nonverbal cues such as nodding and eye contact while they're speaking, and asking questions based on their comments are all indicators of interest and a willingness to assist.

Listening and Inquiring

The reference interview, or inquiry phase, is essential to addressing a patron's actual information need. For example, someone may simply ask for "help with Facebook," without mentioning anything specific. Is this a new user who wants a general overview or is there a specific task he or she wants to complete? Open-ended questions such as "What are you trying to do?" or "What do you want to happen at the end?" are all good ways to engender a more detailed answer and clarify ambiguous requests. Open-ended questions are especially important in an instructional setting because questions about how to use a resource or a device could cover a vast amount of options. Depending on the circumstances, close-ended questions such as "Do you already have an account?" or "Do you know your login information?" are quick ways for instructors to figure out what things they need to address or what they can skip.

Examples of Open-Ended Questions

- What have you already tried?
- What would you like to do or have happen?
- Where did you get stuck?

The tone of the interaction should be positive and encouraging. It is important not to interrupt patrons when they are describing their issue or what they've already done before they came to the library, even if their information is not strictly relevant to their issue. This is because they may think that it's important and essential information that the staff needs in order to help them. Interrupting or negating their experiences may make them self-conscious or they may leave with a feeling that their issue was not fully addressed. With the right questions and the right demeanor, soon "I need help with Facebook" turns into a specific request like "How do I 'un-friend' someone?"

This sample interaction takes place between an adult, online student at a public library who does not have access to his college's physical library and the reference staff. The library only carries popular magazines in print, but they have several databases in which to access journals and articles.

Patron: Where are your journals?

Librarian: What subject do you need?

Patron: Health care.

Librarian: I can show you some online journals that might work. You can even access them from home.

Patron: No. The articles have to be from a print resource and from the past five years.

Librarian: These will count because the articles can come from print journals. I can show you how to tell. We can narrow down the time as well. What's your specific topic, if I may ask?

Patron: I'm looking for how changes in insurance have changed the jobs of healthcare professionals. Mainly doctors.

Librarian: Okay. Let me show you some things that might work. I think trade journals might have some information. Your college library site may have even more. Let me know if you want me to show you that when we're done.

This scenario demonstrated how a patron who was expecting one sort of resource had to be directed to one that he thought was unsuitable. The librarian had to address his need and his qualms, and offer a potentially workable solution by offering to show him how to use the resource. The questions helped the librarian choose the resource, and it let the patron know that he could potentially have all his issues addressed.

Searching

The "searching" part of the process is generally where the instruction occurs and where an individual's learning style preference can fully come into play and affect the transaction. If the patron agrees to the transaction, the instructor can simply ask "Do you want to watch me do it first or do you want to do it and have me talk you through it?" Most people will have a definite preference. This is also the time to offer accompanying handouts, brochures, or other existing material that backs up what is being taught. Writing utensils and paper can be offered to accommodate mechanical learners and the written form of the process can help visual and reading/writing learners. Some people may even say, "I wish there was a video on this," opening the opportunity to offer additional material for them to access on their own. These various accommodations generally take mere moments and can make a large difference in attention span, interest, and retention.

Finding out what patrons already know about their subject will save time and effort during teaching. Are they already familiar with a resource, but it doesn't produce the results they require? Adult learners will quickly abandon resources that don't fulfill their need. If they are having trouble with a process, they can demonstrate what they've already done, reproducing the effect or the problem for the instructor. One example would be someone saying that she is familiar with Google Scholar, but it isn't giving her good results. When asked to demonstrate a search for what she wants, it turns out that she isn't familiar with Boolean operators, so the results are too broad.

Teaching Responsibilities of the eLearning and Instruction Librarian

- Teach member productivity technology classes and support member appointments.
- Provide individual instruction and in the moment access to information in both print and digital formats for all ages.
- Assist individuals with basic technology customer service and instruction.

Example provide by Indian Trails Library,
Public Library District

Encourage the learner throughout the process using both verbal and nonverbal cues and pay attention to the same from the learner. Use positive comments such as "that's right" or "you did it!" and avoid negative phrases such as "no, not like that" or an overt "that's wrong." Instead, use redirecting phrases like "try it this way" or "let's try that again like this. . . ." The learner will pay attention to the instructor's tone and body language as much, and maybe more, than what they say. Nervous or self-conscious patrons may apologize for their ignorance or for taking up someone's time, even if the instructor's verbal and nonverbal cues are warm and inviting. Watch for cues. Folding their arms, not interacting with a device or a process, or frowning are all indicators of confusion or frustration. Sighs, blowing air forcefully out of their nose, and tapping can also be telling indicators. Universal facial expressions and actions such as smiling, nodding, or head-tilting are all signs of understanding and being engaged. Individuals may have their own nonverbal "tells" that differ from the previous examples. The instructor can always ask, if unsure of the patron's nonverbal cues, whether he is following along or how he feels.

Telephone and virtual instruction have built-in limiters in that the librarian might be missing verbal or nonverbal cues to ascertain comfort, understanding, or satisfaction. Walking someone through instruction over the phone provides the opportunity for a conversation, which means that questions and tone can all be used to great effect, even without visual aids. If there is a visual element needed (e.g., "Click on the box. The red box. It should be in the upper-right corner"), it may prove challenging for the instructor if the caller is predominantly a visual learner. If there is an opportunity to follow along, aping the actions of the person on the phone, it can help clarify needs, issues, and directions. Instructional e-mail or chat sessions allow staff to send screenshots, lists, webpages, videos, or other material that the recipient can use to address the issue.

Depending on the library layout and the learner, there may be physical issues, policy barriers, or technical issues to be addressed. Are they able to stand or do they need to sit due to mobility issues? Is there a place where both parties can sit if necessary? Is there an outlet nearby for those who have a device that needs to be plugged because of battery or operation needs? Are patrons allowed to touch staff computers? If not, are there patron-facing computers that will work instead? This can be a serious consideration for a highly mechanical learner. Creating work-arounds and alternatives where possible and making them part of staff training will ensure that each patron's particular issue and need can still be accommodated while keeping to library policy.

Follow-up

Adult learners are satisfied with an instructional encounter when they feel like they've learned what they needed to do what they need to accomplish. If possible, having them reproduce the desired skill or search will show both the instructor and the learners that they are capable and have, in fact, "learned." If any written instructions, brochures, or applicable handouts exist but were not part of the session, make sure they are offered and that they contain the library's contact information. Some learners may feel some trepidation upon leaving the session, nervous of their abilities away from a source of aid. All individuals, no matter the method of contact, should be encouraged to contact the library if they experience any issues when they try it themselves or to return for more assistance.

LIBRARY POLICY AND INSTRUCTION

Libraries have varying expectations and policies regarding the involvement and extent of instruction. It may be that specific employees or departments, such as librarians or computer area staff are designated to address certain topics or even undertake any form of instruction. Some libraries have created specific instructional positions to address community needs above and beyond bibliographic instruction and might have "instructional" or "teaching" included in the job title. More frequently, librarians have that duty built directly built into their job description, making it a matter of policy that they engage in instruction for the staff and the public.

Example of instruction time limits built into Shaker Heights Public Library (OH) Book-a-Librarian service:

Book-a-Librarian

Sign up for a personalized session with a librarian. 30 or 50 minute one-on-one sessions are available to help you get what you need from your library.

Whoever is engaging in teaching, library policies or guidelines should exist for various situations between staff and the public such as one-on-one time limits, reference depth limits, or whether staff is allowed to touch a patron's personal property. These parameters should appear on any material that highlights or markets the service to the public and can be used to reinforce policy when someone wants the instructor to spend more time than is allotted or wants them to do more than the service offers. Having an authoritative policy helps staff set reasonable expectations for patrons. This can help when some patrons frequently request the services of a particular staff member because of their familiarity with their issue or their skill in instruction, which may create a burden on staff and schedules. Guidelines can also be useful when, after instruction has concluded, patrons want staff to stay by their side as a safety measure as they practice and work on their particular issue. As instruction becomes more a part of regular library services, creating such guidelines provides structure and support for both staff and patrons.

BIBLIOGRAPHY

Bambaeeroo, Fatemeh, and Nasrin Shokrpour. 2017. "The Impact of the Teachers' Non-Verbal Communication on Success in Teaching." *Journal of Advances in Medical Education & Professionalism* 5 (2): 51–59. https://www-ncbi-nlm-nih-gov.proxy.lib.ohio-state.edu/pmc/articles/PMC5346168/pdf/JAMP-5-51.pdf.

Hays, Lauren. 2014. "Teaching Information Literacy Skills to Nontraditional Learners." *Kansas Library Association College and University Libraries Section Proceedings* 4 (1): 1–6. https://doi.org/10.4148/2160-942X.1036.

Rader, Hannelore B. 1980. "Reference Services as a Teaching Function." https://www.ideals.illinois.edu/bitstream/handle/2142/7126/librarytrendsv29i1i_opt.pdf.

Reference and User Information Services (RUSA). 2016. "Guidelines for Behavioral Performance of Reference and Information Service Providers." http://www.ala.org/rusa/resources/guidelines/guidelinesbehavioral.

Shaker Public Library. n.d. "Book-a-Librarian." *Shaker Heights Public Library Services.* https://shakerlibrary.org/services/book-a-librarian/.

Silipigni Connaway, Lynn. 2013. "The Library in the Life of the User: Engaging with People Where They Live and Learn." *Guidelines for Behavioral Performance of Reference and Information Service Providers.* https://www.oclc.org/content/dam/research/publications/library/2013/connaway-library2020.pdf. A Preprint Chapter from Library 2020: Today's Leading Visionaries Describe Tomorrow's Library.

U.S. Department of Health and Human Services. 2006. *Research-Based Web Design & Usability Guidelines.* Washington, DC. http://www.usability.gov/sites/default/files/documents/guidelines_books.pdf.

NINE

Class and Group Instruction

Library classes and programs are a form of instructive community service that have the potential to reach multiple people at the same time, address needed or popular interests of the community, and allow a longer, more in-depth learning session than might be possible with a one-on-one session. In order to be motivated and retain information, adults need such experiences to be relevant, engaging, respectful, safe, and add to their skills or understanding (McGrath 2009, 99–110). Instructor, presenter, lecturer, teacher, librarian, whatever title is used, their job is not only to provide class content but also to facilitate an environment where learning can occur. An excellent awareness of community needs, planning and instructional design, public speaking skills, soft skills, and knowledge of the needs and make up of adult learners can make any library class a transformative and enjoyable experience.

INSPIRATION AND FUNDING

Library classes and programs can cover limitless subjects, but should ultimately reflect the needs and interests of your community. Inspiration can (and should) come from frequently asked patron questions, such as how to download e-books, how to write a resume, or frequent requests for genealogy research tips. Libraries can track these questions, interactions, and topics by creating "frequently asked questions" forms either on paper or on a shared form such as Excel or a shared Google Doc. This information over time can turn anecdotal evidence into hard data and shows a picture of what the public wants and needs. One-on-one sessions, which allow for a personal dialogue about experiences and interests, may reveal a gap in local area information or a user population of which the library was unaware. Direct requests or suggestions for a particular class subject, such as smartphone photography or how to value antiques, can create high-interest, high-attendance programs that the public may not have even known were an option. High circulation of particular book topics, such as a real estate or local history, is a clear indicator of local interest. National, state, and local library associations can have resources directly associated with helping libraries create effective programming, such as the "Programming Resources" page found in the "Professional Tools" section of the ALA website (2018).

Classes and programs always have a cost, even if it's just in staff time and preparation. Grant and other funding opportunities exist from the private sector to government agencies that can provide the funds for technology or equipment. Several agencies, such as the Institute of Museum and Library Services (IMLS), or even library-related businesses, such as EBSCO, maintain pages that list grants applicable to libraries (2017, 2018). Depending on the funding rules, these can cover costs for technology and equipment, class resources such as books or printing, and even fund speaker fees for those who want to bring in an outside speaker or pay for extra staff time. Some programs don't need an initial outlay, instead making use of existing library resources and staff knowledge or volunteers from the community.

PREPARATION AND PLANNING

Unlike one-on-ones, where there is no way to know what topic someone may want to learn, classes provide the library the opportunity to choose exactly what they want to present. The topic, the content, the structure, the minimum and maximum number of attendees, all of these are up to the library, but careful planning is needed to ensure an effective and enjoyable program. A well-thought-out outline, synopsis, or worksheet that lists the description, cost, resources, dates, and learning outcomes can serve as a proposal as well as a planning tool. Like a class handout, an application of instructional design, such as the ADDIE model, can ensure that there is a clear and steady progression from concept to execution.

The program designer should be able to answer some basic questions regarding the course, both as a rationale to give it and in order to answer interested inquiries from the public. What is the topic? Who is the intended audience? Why should the library give the class? How long will it be? What are the learning objectives? How will they learn it? What's the class format and setup? Are there ways to address special needs or accommodations? Are there any library resources that can be used in class or that people can use to continue their education after class? What resources will the instructor need to give the class? How much will they cost? Is there a cost to patrons? Will there be a handout? Who creates the handout? Who will be teaching? What are their qualifications? How will class evaluations take place? A methodical review of questions such as these can streamline thoughts and ideas in both the creation and promotion of library classes.

The title and program description are especially important in the creation and implementation of classes and programming. Some libraries create programming brochures or calendars that get distributed beyond the library walls. Other potential attendees will discover class opportunities via online searches. The title and description should be immediately indicative of who should attend and what they'll learn. It should speak to the adult learner's desire to learn, fix a problem, address a need or interest, or enhance their life. It should also answer immediate questions such as how to sign up (if necessary), where it will be held, when it occurs, and what someone will need to bring (if applicable). Highlighting an experienced or well-known speaker in your promotions can also draw in attendees who desire to learn from an acknowledged expert.

Class format and room settings have a great influence on program planning and on how people learn. There are a variety of presentation and instructional formats in which a class can take place. One option is workshops, where participants interact hands-on with the topic that involves a process or workflow. These work well with technology, software, crafts, life skills, or other task-oriented activities. Lectures, where a speaker presents an informational topic (and not a process) in front of a class, generally have a potential for a larger group. Some examples that suit a lecture format might include a local history lecture, a presentation on news-relevant science such as global warming or plate tectonics, or personal accounts such as a refugee's personal story. Social issues such as healthcare, education, or homeless populations, politics, and other potentially controversial topics may be well-suited to a discussion format that is moderated by the class instructor. Participants are given the chance to present a side or argument on a given topic and contrast it against, and learn, from each other's perspectives.

The following example details the application of the ADDIE model, an instructional design process, in the creation of a class on how to start plants from seed (see Figure 7.1).

Analyze

Local stores are starting to give paid classes to learn how to plant seeds following a local "green" movement. Related books and media have seen an increase in circulation. The goal is to have a hands-on class that teaches people how to start seeds indoors that they will later plant in a garden or in containers. The class should be scheduled before or during seed-starting season for the zone six growing area. The intended audience is inexperienced, would-be adult gardeners who can't afford to pay for a similar class. It will be a lecture and demonstration format followed by a hands-on activity. Participants will plant seeds in small containers and take them home after the class. The class should take an hour and a half.

Design

The size of the room and the consideration of space for activities limit the class to ten participants. The learning objectives will be that participants will (1) learn where to look on a seed packet for planting instructions such as when to plant, planting depth, spacing, and seedling instructions; (2) soil and seed starter information and needs; (3) seedling or planting container considerations for indoors; (4) lighting, heating, and watering information; and (5) how to separate and replant seedlings into new containers. The instructional strategy will be to have a lecture (audio learners) and demonstration on seed packet information and a run-through of the planting process using a YouTube video or GIF (visual learners), a discussion of what seeds need to grow, and a demonstration on how to plant seeds. Everyone will then plant seeds from seed packs into containers of soil starter, both of which have been donated by the local gardening club (mechanical learners). They will then plant sprouted seedlings into the other half of the tray to learn that process. They will take home the tray along with a sheet detailing the processes that they practiced as well as what to do for the next step (read/writing learners).

Develop

The class will be given by a staff member with gardening experience, a local garden center employee, or a member of the local gardening club.

Class resources include: laptop, projector, screen, tables, chairs, ten eight-by-eight aluminum foil trays, seed starter soil, paper cups of seedlings, five seed packs, a grow light or bulb, and paper towels. The information for the course will come from applicable net resources on seed-starting and gardening information for the zone six growing area. Videos will be shown to demonstrate planting processes so that everyone has a clear view. The video or a GIF will be put on loop during the activity to provide a visual aid. There will be two people per table, with class resources split between them, including soil starter, seed packs, paper cups of seedlings, and water. The germination timing will be based on the plant.

Implement

Create a title and class description for marketing purposes before marketing deadlines. Reserve the room and necessary equipment. Purchase necessary items. Create a "How to Start Seeds Indoors" instruction sheet that contains pictures and a numbered list (two pages maximum). Make a list of local gardening agencies and a recommended reading or viewing list for more information. Create a presentation that consists of a PowerPoint presentation with links and videos. Write a script and practice the class to figure out timing and possible questions. Cultivate seeds beforehand to have seedlings available for the class. Have a coworker with no gardening experience run through the activity section to gauge timing needs and potential questions. Create a class evaluation form for participant feedback.

Evaluate

Share the class plan and content with coworkers for feedback. Adjust procedure or content as necessary. During class, gauge participant reaction and perceptions. Participant satisfaction will be based on whether they believe they can reproduce the results at home. Use class observations along with class evaluations to make needed modifications for future classes.

This method can be used for any potential project, ensuring the efficient and effective use of library resources and instructor talent.

A GOOD TEACHER

A good teacher assures participants through their words and actions that they are knowledgeable and capable of assisting with their acquisition of skills and knowledge while keeping the class learner-centered (Fein and

Logan 2003, 47). They control the environment to the extent that the promised content gets covered in the specified amount of time and that the class setting remains conducive to learning. Common examples of this would be addressing those who are on their phone and causing a disturbance or finding ways redirect or stop the "talker" who wants to share their own personal story concerning the topic at every opportunity. Teachers can build in guidelines and expectations at the beginning of class regarding asking questions, cell phone usage, and even telling participants that they may have to redirect discussions or activities in order to keep the class on track.

An engaging and effective teacher can help all learners better connect with the material and feel more confident in their new knowledge and skills. This can be done by sharing examples and illustrations of how the information relates to or helps participants, essentially reminding them why they are there and how they can benefit from the instruction. An example of this at the beginning of a six-person photography class would be a teacher asking everyone to give an example of what they don't like about their past photos (e.g., always too dark) and then sharing what aspect of the class might address their issue (e.g., lighting for different environments). Some teachers will actively ask students how they feel they learn best (i.e., their learning style) and then relate how the class will accommodate their needs. The following example shows how these features are highlighted during the introductions:

> For those of you who like to learn by doing, we'll be practicing what we learn in the second half of the class. Those of you who like to watch the process before you try it, I'll run through it a few times beforehand and then I'll have an example video running while all of you practice. Everything that we're doing is written down on this sheet, so you'll have something to refer to when you go home. Feel free to ask me to repeat anything you might need.

The instructor generally never knows beforehand what kinds of learners are going to come to class, but a combination of strong presentation skills, competency in the subject, observation of and empathy for the students, and a genuine interest that participants learn all contribute to the making of a great teacher.

Instruction is a form of public speaking and many of the attributes of a good public speaker are tied to active listening skills. Planning is an important element, ensuring that the teacher is familiar with the intended audience and their potential needs, the learning objectives, and the process or progression that the class is supposed to take. A teacher pays attention to the verbal and nonverbal body language of the audience and adjusts the material accordingly, spending more time or offering clarification on confusing points. If there is a demonstration or other activity that necessitates the instructor turn away from the students, they purposefully look up and observe the crowd when possible. They ask open-ended questions to gauge understanding and make participants actively think about the material and apply it to themselves. They pause at intervals to specifically ask to make sure that people are following along or on task, allaying anxiety where possible. They give concrete examples and illustrations that give the information context and applicability. Teachers will also summarize key points during the class, tying the class information back to the point of the class and the needs of the participants.

A teacher's mannerism and preparedness can have a marked effect on the class. Students may be paying attention to the teacher as they present information and give demonstrations, but the actual focus and purpose of any class is that they learn. A nervous presenter who is disorganized in thought and class material can lose the confidence of the participants and make them more aware of the teacher than the class content. The teacher's attitude about the topic, such as whether they find it boring, elementary, or wildly interesting, will generally come across as well. Opinions and attitudes about students, like a willingness to help those who lag behind or an impatience for the same, are also usually readily evident to all in the class. Enthusiasm and interest can be contagious, but so can any negative emotions and comments. A positive verbal and nonverbal attitude about the topic and the student's abilities to learn will set the tone for the whole class.

A prepared and knowledgeable instructor will realize that everyone has different learning styles and comes to class with differing levels of experience. That means that each class will have its own rhythm and progression through the material, which will require patience and flexibility from the instructor. The presentation should accommodate as many learning types as possible through class materials, visual aids, and the use of clear, jargon-free language. Time should be built in to every program for questions and answers, with the instructor giving verbal permission and encouragement at the beginning of the class to ask questions. Some instructors, especially in a lecture format, may request that questions wait until after a presentation. The problem with this process is that many individuals will forget their question by the end. Questions throughout, even if it's at timed intervals or at the end of a particular subject, will allow people to clarify points for understanding and not lose their question to forgetfulness or information overload. If a question is not pertinent to the class and could potentially confuse or sidetrack others, the student can be politely redirected to ask at another time (i.e., "see me after class and I can tell you all about that"). If that question will be answered at a later point in the discussion, simply say so. Participants generally benefit from other attendee's questions; the clarification solidifying information, or potentially answering a question that someone else didn't want to ask. The instructor should learn from each experience and reflect on their own attitude, skills, class processes, and class content, making adjustments wherever necessary in order to improve the next endeavor.

CONSIDERING THE STUDENT

According to the self-directed aspect of adult learning theory, no matter the skills or will of the teacher, in the end the student has the most influence over how much they take away from a class. Whatever need or interest brought them through the doors, there are several factors that can affect how and if they'll learn the material as well as how they'll feel about the experience. The teacher is one element to consider, but other factors include the class format and materials, the physical environment, and other students. If you want your classes to be useful and well-attended, give each of these factors serious consideration. Not only will those who had a good experience come back for more but also they will advertise their experience (the good and the bad) to friends, family, and potentially the world via social media.

Andragogy Principles

- Self-directed learner
- Utilizes knowledge and life experiences
- Learning is goal- or relevancy-oriented
- Aware of the gap
- Class is secondary
- Internal and external motivators

Alewine 2010, 11

Students readily demonstrate principles of andragogy when they attend a library class or program, and there's a direct link between an adult's attitude, emotions, and motivation to learn, all of which they will bring with them to class (Alewine 2010, 11). Adults are self-directed learners, meaning that they are responsible for their own learning. Because few library classes have tests or quizzes and are mostly one-shot classes instead of a series, it's up to the learner to evaluate their progress. They'll be consciously aware of whether they "learned" anything. Learners will come from a vast array of life experiences and situations. Even if they know nothing about the subject at hand, other things that they know or have experienced will have an impact on what and how they learn. This also brings the unique opportunity for students potentially to help or learn from each other. The teacher can capitalize on this by suggesting that students ask questions of each other and by inviting input during and after class.

Adult "learning," according to one adult education theorist, is a process in which students move from the acquisition of information to utilizing it in their thought processes and actions (Illeris 2002, 19–20). This is a multistep process that starts with experience, which can be the interaction with the information, either formally or informally. In a library class, this includes both the class material and the information or experience that the student already possesses. An example of this would be someone who comes to a class about cloud storage. They are adept at physical forms of storage (hard drives and flash drives) and they know there's a connection, but they don't know what cloud storage is and they've been told it's the best way to handle their computer archives, so they're taking the class.

After experience, the next step is participation, where the students interact with the information in a way that explains it and puts it into context. This step helps them personally associate with the information and start to compare it to what they already know. An example of this would be having the students move files from the computer or a flash drive to a cloud storage system, such as Google Drive. Internalization and integration of the material follows, where the information is now understood and paired, schema-wise, with similar information and processes that can be applied to other contexts. This moment in class would be having them sign out of all their accounts and then having them perform all the sign-in, file moving, file naming, access, and retrieval steps on their own to prove that they know it. This same process can apply to programs that are not skill-based as well by using open-ended questions and engaging the audience in the topic.

Most adults who engage in a class or program are goal-oriented. They are coming to learn something from this particular class because they need it. The purely curious and interested adults still exhibit andragogical principles. They didn't have to come. They, too, are expecting to learn the subject matter, which is an immediate goal. Relevancy is the walk away proof (mentally) that they learned something. It can be a skill, but it can also be a realization of broadened understanding or clarity. Not many adult learners will go to a class if they think that they already know the information. They are aware of the knowledge gap and they're trying to fill it. This is important to remember, since the class or program at the library is secondary to other things in their lives.

Every adult learner has internal or external motivators as to why they are attending. Internal, or intrinsic, motivation refers to doing something because it is enjoyable or interesting (Ryan and Deci 2000, 55). External, or extrinsic, motivation is when there is a desired outcome or even a consequence if something doesn't take place. An example of this would be people who are in the same word-processing class but for different reasons. The externally motivated students have been told by their employers that they need to know the software if they hope for a raise or company advancement. The internally motivated students are looking forward to the material so that they can create their own family greeting cards or other documents. Both externally and internally motivated students have desired outcomes that will utilize information from the class, but their attitudes and emotions about it may be very different in that the externally motivated student may feel pressured or resentful. If the class size permits, the instructor can ask participants why they are there and how they hope to apply the information. If the class is too large, it can be included as a question during registration or as part of the class evaluation at the end. Their answers can serve as concrete examples throughout the class that help connect the information to the reason they are there in the first place.

Internal/Intrinsic Motivators	External/Extrinsic Motivators
Self-perception	Competition
Curiosity	Fear of consequence
Love	Money
Personal fulfillment	Rewards
A desire to learn	Praise

THE LEARNING ENVIRONMENT

The class environment, including layout, lighting, temperature, and acoustics can all affect the learner's experience to the point that it affects their ability to learn. Anyone who has ever attended an event where they couldn't hear the presenter, were cold or hot the entire time, were seated in uncomfortable chairs, or couldn't see will attest that they didn't benefit much from the experience. These distractions, whether they were just irritants or actual barriers, can derail the entire experience and prevent participants from ever returning. Some common environmental factors can include:

- Sound: acoustics, ambient noise, the instructor's voice
- Temperature: heating and cooling, ventilation
- Lighting: too much or too little
- Tables and seating: setup (circles vs. rows), comfort, space to work, and proximity to other students
- Room aesthetics: décor and materials from other classes or groups being left in the room

Classroom aids such as microphones, multidirectional sound systems, and patron listening devices can help address sound issues. Ambient noise might come from ventilation, adjoining rooms, or spaces outside the learning space. Some simple solutions include closing the door and taking care that a potentially noisy program, such as a children's story time, doesn't coincide with the class. If the sounds are unavoidable, white noise or noise-cancellation machines can help reduce ambient noise inside the classroom. Building considerations, such as lighting, temperature, and décor may be harder to address, but if circumstances warrant, recommendations for attire can be made in the event description. A learning space that contains materials from other groups or activities can seem unprofessional, cluttered, or distracting for class participants. Instructors should take the opportunity to practice in the event space so that they're potentially aware of these factors.

Emotional considerations have a direct link to cognition and can encompass things like self-image, comfort level, shyness, and doubt (Nelken 2009, 184–85). Imagine if someone in their seventies comes to a smartphone class, but everybody else in the class is in their twenties. Before class even starts, they may have some feelings about their ability to keep up. The same might be true if reversed in that a twenty-something year-old might feel slightly shamed that they're at the same tech level, skill-wise, as a senior. If during the class, someone feels like they're falling behind, they may often give up and disengage mentally and emotionally from the instruction. This is why observing body language and expressions is so important for the instructor.

The instructor won't know where everyone is coming from emotionally, but they do have to be aware that such feelings can affect how someone learns and allay possible anxieties as they come up. Age-related anxieties may be allayed by marketing classes directly toward certain age groups, such as "for seniors" or "for new adults." Commending participant's interest and effort at the beginning of class may help sooth anxiety. A class in anything for beginners can start with a simple, "I expect you to know nothing about this subject," which may dispel fears about what they think they are supposed to know or what is expected from them. Inviting questions and clarifications at the outset (e.g., "you're here to learn, so ask me questions if you get stuck or don't understand" or "make sure to ask questions if you have them, because someone else is probably wondering the same thing") can remove the fear that keeps some people from asking questions. Close-ended questions (e.g., "Did it work?" or "Who needs help?") may be useful in activity-based classes to discover who might be lagging behind or having trouble. Most learning situations benefit more from open-ended questions (e.g., "How would you use what you just learned?" or "What are some questions that you still have after covering this?").

MURPHY'S LAW IN THE CLASSROOM

The best way to deal with potential classroom issues is to prepare ahead of time and have a plan of action for when they occur. And they will. Behavioral issues, software malfunctions, equipment and building problems, and even staffing issues all have the potential to make the classroom a less than optimal learning environment. While most patrons are understanding and sympathetic to the plight of the instructor, they are expecting the issue to be addressed so that the class can continue.

Behavioral issues may come in many forms that are all the responsibility of the instructor to rectify or address. This could include contentious participants, "talkers" who are causing a distraction and making it hard to hear or concentrate, phone calls or other device distractions, or someone who is manipulating classroom time or discussions. One way to address these is to state expectations at the very outset. Since everyone hears the "rules," they are forming a kind of "social contract," agreeing to that contract by the fact that they stay (Nelken 2009, 182). Here is an example of an opening statement (social or class contract) at the beginning of a workshop for how to write personal memoirs that lists what the class can expect from the teacher and what the teacher expects from the students.

> Hello everyone and thank you for coming. Today we're going to cover common elements of personal memoirs, how to take notes on personal interviews, and what legal considerations might apply to writing about other people. I'll have examples on the screen, which also appear on your handout. Raise your hand if you need me to go over something again. You are here to learn, after all. You can ask me questions at any time, but if time gets tight, I may ask you to see me after class so that we can make sure to cover all of the material. If we have time at the end you may be able to share some of your own experiences with the rest of the class. This room is pretty small, but let me know if you have any trouble seeing or hearing anything and I'll see what I can do. Please take a moment to turn off the ringer or sound to your device. If you're not sure if it is on or how to do that, raise your hand and I'll do it for you then we can get started.

This example took mere minutes to say, but it covers the roles of both the teacher and the students and addresses multiple potential behavioral issues that could affect the progression of the class as well as the attention and comfort of other students.

If behavioral issues still occur, the teacher should address them promptly in a firm, friendly manner. For example, if someone still takes a phone call during class, the teacher can smile and quietly remind them that they'll have more privacy if they step outside the class. If two people are talking to each other and causing a distraction, the teacher can pause and genuinely ask them if they have a question or concern. This lets them know that their behavior is being noticed and is potentially distracting. Instead of singling out an offender, a reminder to the class in general about distractions, talking, or devices may be enough to stop the behavior. If it still persists, the teacher may ask to speak to them privately. In a worst-case scenario, they might have to ask the person to stop the behavior or leave. Staff should be familiar with the situation, policies, and procedures that go along with evicting someone from a class or the library. Even if it causes a minor disruption in class, other participants expect and rely on the instructor or staff to maintain an environment conducive to learning.

Malfunctions in equipment, software, or the physical building can have a significant impact on a class. This is especially true if the technical aspect is the sole means of presenting the information. All class content should be backed up to at least more than one device or storage device when possible. Equipment that has software essential to the class should be regularly tested, especially before the class, to make sure that all components are in working order. Instructors should be aware if and where alternate, accessible equipment is in the library in case replacements are needed. An adequate class setup time should be applied so that if a problem does occur at the last minute, there is enough time to address it before class begins. Many adult classes occur in the evening when there may be no technical support staff available to help, so alternate staff help may be required. Building problems, such as room setup help, temperature issues, or even ceiling leaks or an out-of-order restroom may also create issues of safety, comfort, or access. Fixing these issues may be as simple as contacting maintenance personnel unless the issue can't be addressed in the class timeframe. Preparation, familiarity with the classroom, knowledge of available and alternate equipment, and knowing who might be able to help can help any instructor troubleshoot and resolve problems.

Staffing issues can affect classes as well. Most programs are scheduled months in advance in order to advertise to the public and make sure the space is available for use. Staff changes and call-offs may affect who can give the class and even whether it can occur at all. For example, if an employee who is well-versed in scrapbooking creates a class but leaves the library before the class occurs, the library has to decide whether to still offer the class. Will they ask the staff to see if someone wants to take it on or will they call in an outside expert to make sure that the craft and presentation skills are adequate for a library class? Had they already created class content or will someone else have to do so? If someone else will teach it and the description and schedule are already out for public consumption, care must be taken to keep to the learning objectives that were listed in the description, since that is what participants will be expecting. Classes may also be affected if someone calls off in the library. Even if it's not the instructor, is there adequate desk coverage? Are they now the designated person in-charge so that they might get called out of class to deal with an issue? If it is the instructor, is there someone who is qualified and familiar enough with the material and the class structure who can successfully substitute? Some libraries, such as the Denver Public Library, layout their classes in detail as a sort of map that others can potentially follow to give consistent and reliable classes, no matter who might be teaching (Figure 9.1). If classes do need to be cancelled the same day, it is important that other staff know the procedure on how to inform those who have signed up, hopefully before they arrive. If there was no registration required, appropriate signage should be displayed that apologizes for the inconvenience and directs them to the correct source for more information. If possible, having someone at the designated room location will allow for the chance to explain, apologize, and offer answers to any questions.

Technology for Presentations

Learn how to improve your presentation while using PowerPoint and other presentation software. Explore best practices for designing and delivering your presentation. You'll also get hands-on experience with the hardware used to deliver your presentation.

Learning Objectives

At the end of class, the student will

- Have a basic understanding to create a slide presentation
- Know what software is available for presenting including PowerPoint and Google Slides.
- Know what hardware can be used to deliver a presentation.
- Understand basic best practices for slide design.

Lesson Prep Work

(30 min, at a minimum, prior to student arrival)

- Get in early to test for technology failure, because it will happen :-)
- Pre-sign into accounts, including Gmail to demo Google Slides.
- Pre-sign into Prezi to show short examples.
- Recording a presentation
    - *https://support.office.com/en-us/article/record-a-slide-show-with-narration-and-slide-timings-0b9502c6-5f6c-40ae-b1e7-e47d8741161c#OfficeVersion=2013,_2016*
- If using Keynote, connect iPad to demo.
- Print handouts.
- Get example hardware (VGA, HDMI cables, adapters, clickers)

Figure 9.1. Lesson Plan for "Technology for Presentations" from Denver Public Library

BIBLIOGRAPHY

Alewine, Hollisa S. 2010. "Andragogical Methods and Readiness for the Correctional GED Classroom." *Journal of Correctional Education* 61 (1): 9–22.

American Library Association (ALA). 2018. "Programming Resources." *Publications and Resources*. http://www.ala.org/pla/resources/tools/programming-instruction/programming-resources.

Fein, Adam D., and Mia C. Logan. 2003. "Preparing Instructors for Online Instruction." *New Directions for Adult and Continuing Education* 100: 45–55.

"Grants & Funding Sources for Libraries." 2018. EBSCO Connect, October 26, 2018. https://connect.ebsco.com/s/article/Grants-Funding-Sources-for-Libraries?language=en_US.

Illeris, Knud. 2002. *The Three Dimensions of Learning: Contemporary Learning Theory in the Tension Field between the Cognitive, the Emotional and the Social*. Translated by Dorothy Reader and Margaret Malone. Frederiksberg and Leicester: Roskilde University Press & Niace Publications.

Institute of Museum and Library Services (IMLS). n.d. "Apply for a Grant." https://www.imls.gov/grants/apply-grant/available-grants.

Matteson, Miriam L. 2014. "The Whole Student: Cognition, Emotion, and Information Literacy." *College & Research Libraries* 75 (6): 862–77. https://doi.org/10.5860/crl.75.6.862.

McGrath, Valerie. 2009. "Reviewing the Evidence on How Adult Students Learn: An Examination of Knowles' Model of Andragogy." *Adult Learner: The Irish Journal of Adult and Community Education*: 99–110. https://files.eric.ed.gov/fulltext/EJ860562.pdf.

Nelken, Melissa L. 2009. "Negotiating Classroom Process: Lessons from Adult Learning." *Negotiation Journal* 25 (April): 181–94.

Newman, Michael. 2012. "Calling Transformative Learning into Question: Some Mutinous Thoughts." *Adult Education Quarterly* 62 (1): 36–55. http://aeq.sagepub.com.

Ryan, Richard M., and Edward L. Deci. 2000. "Intrinsic and Extrinsic Motivations: Classic Definitions and New Directions." *Contemporary Educational Psychology* 25: 54–67.

Scofield, Jim. 1997. "Learning Environments for Adult Learners: Implications for Teacher Development." *The Catesol Journal* 10 (1): 121–27. https://eric.ed.gov/?id=ED432924.

TEN

Online Teaching

Online, self-directed learning is becoming more common in business training, formal education, and self-help as the tech-savvy public more fully integrates technology and instant access into their lives. "Online" for this chapter is defined specifically as video-based content that potential learners can see or hear about a tutorial, demonstration, or other information. Patrons whose first instinct or preference is to learn on their own or go immediately online to seek instruction are accustomed to high-quality content, easily accessible from a multitude of company sites or video hosting websites such as YouTube, Vimeo, or the Internet Archive. This "on-demand" need for information and education has influenced many libraries as they evaluate, integrate, and create instructional content for the public.

ONLINE LEARNING

Advantages	Disadvantages
Convenient	Needs Internet access
Self-paced	Requires computer and internet competency
Consistent quality	Potential information overload
Accessible anywhere	Lack of Q&A for clarity
More content choice	
Repeatable	

Libraries and library vendors have recognized the value of online tutorials and its ability to reach larger audiences. They have responded with databases and content that appeal to and accommodate a variety of skill levels and learning types. Library products such as Gale's Testing & Education Reference Center, EBSCO's LearningExpress Library, and LinkedIn's Lynda.com all offer professional, expert-led videos on an endless array of topics such as interview skills, common software tutorials, professional test preparation, and others that address common adult needs and topics. These databases and their high-quality content are generally only accessible to the public with the use of a library card.

Software and product companies regularly create their own branded tutorials and instructional material, placing them on their own websites but also on popular video hosting sites. A Google search for a product name and the word "tutorial" can easily produce millions of results, from videos created by the owning company to amateurs filming in their basements. Viewers, like an in-person student, will have definite preferences as to the visual production, timing, the content, and even the presenter that will make them choose one video over another.

Much of this valuable content is now regularly used by library staff to answer reference questions and to offer as a tool for instruction. In-person offers of a video that answers a question or teaches a skill may be met with either joy or trepidation depending on someone's comfort, access, and learning style. If access is not an issue, highlighting the visual and audio aspects will appeal to those types of learners. Those who might not be as comfortable with the format may be won over when shown that they can replay a video as many times as they want until they "get it," something that can't always be done face-to-face. Most web-based videos are able to be sent via link to an e-mail, making them applicable to most reference situations. Even during a phone transaction, a quick "I can send you a video that shows you what to do" can help those who might be frustrated with a lack of visual aid.

Videos can be embedded in library classes and public presentations that provide examples, explanations, or demonstrations depending on the topic. With proper permission and citation, vetted material could conceivably be embedded in a library website, hyper-linked and tagged to appear on applicable searches as a way to connect users to appropriate and library-recommended content. These methods hold with a public library's role to provide information and learning opportunities to the public and remain relevant in a rapidly changing world.

While the Internet holds a seemingly endless array of free learning opportunities for adults, some topics may not be available as a teaching tool or they may cost the public money to access. Some location-specific topics might include local history information, common local government issues such as healthcare process, new business information, or local tourism. Libraries also have the opportunity to create online literacy instruction that is specific to the library's own populations and library resources. An example of this would be a video for would-be entrepreneurs that walks viewers through the steps involving the local chamber of commerce as well as highlighting library resources, such as marketing and legal form databases. There are many situations where the library has the opportunity to create original online content and address the information and instructional needs of their specific community.

CREATING ONLINE CONTENT

Before your library creates online videos and tutorials, you need to consider certain factors and answer some questions. First, use online instruction best practice principles as a way to determine whether to record your live classes or create online-only classes (Blummer and Kritskaya 2009, 201). Conduct a needs assessment to ascertain possible local user groups and interested parties and gauge whether your patrons are actually utilizing similar library resources. The fact that such content can be accessed by any possible user online doesn't change the fact that your library's resources and efforts should primarily benefit the community you serve. Another important consideration is whether your library has the staff interest, ability, time, and resources to produce a quality video.

Images and other proprietary content used in a presentation must be properly cited and credited and permissions should be granted if content is copyrighted, or their appearance on a publicly viewed site can draw potential legal action against the library. Outside speakers may not want their program, for which they might be being paid and hope to market to others, put out for free public consumption. Most hold the rights to their class or program unless expressly stated otherwise in their contract, meaning that if the library expressly wants to record the class and retain the rights, they may have to pay extra for it. Patrons, too, may not appreciate being in a class where their voice, if nothing else could be recorded, stifling any question that they might have asked. Careful camera placement may ensure that no one but the speaker appears on film, but the mere presence of the equipment may intimidate or disrupt someone's learning ability. Stating that a recording will take place in the description can help avoid a potentially unpleasant surprise when people get to class. Like any instructional design process, careful planning from start to finish prevents issues in production as well as liability.

If there is so much applicable, quality content available through databases or online, why should a library consider recording classes and programs or creating their own online tutorials? One reason is that not all of the programs or instructional materials that a library produces are reflective or available online. Some libraries don't have the funds to purchase tutorial databases such as those mentioned above. Others may not have the website capabilities to embed or link to external content. Creating content is also a way to ensure that, like an in-person situation, all possible accommodations are made to address the needs of learning styles, possible levels of understanding, and answering a specific question or problem.

Some of the most valuable and original content that your library can produce has to do with your own unique community. Local history, personal experiences and success stories, and other unique subjects mean that certain programs and accounts can only exist in that particular spot on Earth. These one-of-a-kind programs might stand as a form of oral history, provide a resource for local school systems, or serve as the basis for discussion-type programming where attendees view the video and then discuss it in class. Memoir-like programs, where a speaker details his or her personal experience or point of view, often have a high turnout, reflecting the popularity of print biographies and memoirs.

The popularity of National Public Radio's (NPR) StoryCorp, an endeavor that records the stories and experiences of everyday people and makes the recordings available online, attests the potential interest on an online audience (NPR, n.d.). The Center for Digital Storytelling (CDS), an organization that collaborates with partners to produce and present personal stories that address social issues, suggests seven steps to assist in the telling and recording of personal narratives (Lambert 2010, 9–24; Blithe, Carrera, and Medaille 2015, 61–62):

1. Offer a point of view that's unique to the presenter.
2. Begin with a dramatic question and then answer or resolve the question by the end of the narrative.
3. Use true, emotional elements to highlight the impact of the experience.

4. Employ the "gift of the voice" or how the speaker's voice reflects their personal connection to the story.

5. Use the "power of the soundtrack" or the use of music to enhance the emotional content of the story.

6. Create a concise, economic retelling and the use of well-chosen images to connect viewers with the material.

7. Control the pacing of the story, using a natural, progressive rhythm to maintain the interest of the audience.

These elements can help engage listeners and invest them in a story that has the potential to teach history, life-lessons, culture, perspective, and other information that can enrich lives and spread understanding.

Another reason to create online content is to meet specific local user group needs and interests. Conduct a needs assessments. For example, a class for online nursing students might highlight relevant library resources, such as nursing test prep books, interlibrary services, or databases that feature medical journals, and other library databases. The class could outline basic research strategies and cover a demonstration of Google Docs and Microsoft's OneDrive as resources for paper writing. The same could be done for those interested in genealogy or local history. The class could outline research strategies, library holdings for genealogy resources, and contact information for local interest groups. These types of instructional videos would essentially serve as pathfinders, or advertisements and guides to library resources and services that pertain specifically to a particular user group.

RECORDING AND PRESENTATION OPTIONS

Recording Live and Live Streaming

Recording live refers here to recording a class or program that is being given to the public and involves the use of a camera, camcorder, or other recording device such as a tablet or smartphone to film the speaker, screens, and demonstrations. These recordings may be edited after the fact to remove background noise, verbal pauses, class breaks, or participant's voices. Editing a video requires knowledge of media editing software in order to create a quality product. Recordings can also be used as is, the rationale being that the viewer will then have the same experience as those who attended in person, benefiting from all of the verbal and nonverbal cues from the instructor as well as the questions posed by in-house attendees. Adding any downloadable class handouts or links to resource lists to the page featuring the video will give viewers access to the same material and tools as those who attended, increasing the availability of the information and opening up the content to multimodal users.

Live streaming is when a class is being recorded and presented online at the same time. Depending on the platform, online viewers may be able to interact with the speaker and ask questions in real-time or leave feedback after the class is over. Some live stream services include Facebook Live, YouTube Live Streaming, Instagram, and Open Broadcaster Software (Moreau 2018). Some streaming services may also be able to "capture" the video as it progresses. When the class ends (or the recording stops) the live stream is archived as a viewable video.

Equipment can be as simple or as complicated (read also as expensive) as the library desires. Live streaming necessitates an Internet capable recording device and software along with a strong Internet connection. Basic recording will use a camera or other recording device. A tripod is recommended for all recording devices to ensure stability while recording and placement that doesn't interfere with participants while at the same time allowing for a shot that encompasses all needed material. Depending on the ambient noise, the quality of the recording device, and the voice of the speaker, a microphone might be necessary to ensure audio quality in the video. The microphone could be part of the room's inherent sound system or could be a separate unit that connects to the recording device. Wireless models that clip to clothing near the speaker's collar are one of the best ways to ensure clarity. Lighting is another important consideration given the visual nature of video. Not only does it allow for the clear view of presented material and demonstrations, but it also allows the viewer to fully appreciate and apply the body language of the instructor to the material.

Online Presentations and Screen Capture

Online tutorials, classes, and prevalence of recorded webinars and seminars speak to the popularity, accessibility, and applicability of presenting in an online, passive format. Video editing software can be used to combine images and audio files to produce a video that delivers the same in-person class content and learning objects to a virtual audience. According to *PC Magazine's* "Editor's Choice," the best video editing software of 2018 included products such as Adobe Premiere, Apple Final Cut Pro X, Corel VideoStudio Ultimate, CyberLink PowerLink, and Apple iMovie (Muchmore 2018). On the other side of the price spectrum, budget-minded libraries, or those who want a chance to hone their editing skills before paying, still have access to free editing software. TechRadar.com rated the best free video editors as Lightworks, Hitfilm, Shortcut, and VSDC Free Video Editor (Ellis 2018).

Screen capture is software that records the contents and movements of a computer screen and mouse and then turns it into a(n audio-less) video. This utility is built into an Apple Mac's Quick Time Player's "screen record" function and is available for download (some free and some paid) for most devices. Microsoft's PowerPoint program, besides being one of the most common class content creation and presentation tools, has the ability to record audio, add sound effects and animation, create timings, and then convert the entire product into a video.

No matter the quality of a video, it is only truly useful if people can find it. Relevant titles, keyword tags, and link placement to the video are all paramount to the public being able to independently find and access the library's video. Whether it's on the library website or on an external hosting site, the video title should reflect the class topic and learning objectives as they are more likely to show up in the search results. For example, a class titled "Microsoft Word Tutorial: Adjusting Fonts and Spacing" tells the viewer the topic, that it's instructive, and specifically what they'll learn. The description provides further details and, in many cases, acts as a searchable field on the site for other associated keywords. A library video on a site such as YouTube is competing with potentially millions of other videos based on keyword searches. Embedding the video on the library site allows for more brand recognition, associating the content and services with the library and makes it possible to keep information seekers on the library's website where they might find a variety of associated tools and resources.

As technology continues to evolve, libraries may find even more opportunities to share their instructional expertise and resources with the public. This online form of embedded librarianship, where library services and talent are brought to the user, allows the library to reach and assist people far beyond the building and time restrictions of the physical library (Silipigni Connaway 2015, 202–3).

BIBLIOGRAPHY

Blithe, Sarah Jane, Winter Carrera, and Ann Medaille. 2015. "Stories of Service-Learning: Guidelines for Increasing Student Engagement with Digital Storytelling." *Journal of Library Innovation* 6, no. 1 (January): 60–74.

Blummer, B. A., and O. Kritskaya. 2009. "Best Practices for Creating an Online Tutorial: A Literature Review." *Journal of Web Librarianship* 3: 199–216.

Connaway, Lynn Silipigni. 2015. "The Library in 2020 Will Be Engagement-Centered." *The Library in the Life of the User: Engaging with People Where They Live and Learn*, 202–7. Dublin, OH: OCLC Research. http://www.oclc.

Ellis, Cat. 2018. "The Best Video Editing Software 2018." *TechRadar*. https://www.techradar.com/news/best-video-editing-software-paid-and-free.

Facebook Live. Facebook. https://live.fb.com/.

Lambert, Joe. 2010. *Digital Storytelling Cookbook*. Berkeley, CA: Digital Diner Press.

Microsoft Support. n.d. "Publish Your PowerPoint Slide Show as a Video to YouTube—PowerPoint." https://support.office.com/en-us/article/publish-your-powerpoint-slide-show-as-a-video-to-youtube-ab3e03fd-a0fd-46aa-8d4d-4ac0bf62fd5b.

Moreau, Elise. 2018. "10 Popular Tools for Broadcasting Live Video Online." *Lifewire*. https://www.lifewire.com/tools-for-broadcasting-live-video-3486110.

Muchmore, Michael. 2018. "Best Video Editing Software 2018—Lab Tested Reviews by PCMag.Com." *PC Magazine*. https://www.pcmag.com/article2/0,2817,2397215,00.asp.

National Public Radio (NPR). n.d. *StoryCorps*. https://storycorps.org/.

Nijboer, Jelke, and Esther Hammelburg. 2010. "Extended Media Literacy: A New Direction for Libraries." *New Library World* 111 (5): 36–45. https://doi.org/https://doi.org/10.1108/03074801011015676.

Open Broadcaster Software. n.d. *OBS Studio*. https://obsproject.com/.

YouTube Live Streaming. *YouTube*. https://support.google.com/youtube/answer/2474026?hl=en.

ELEVEN

Outside Instructors

Hiring outside instructors and speakers for classes or programs is an effective way to engage the community's interest, access local talent, and build the library's reputation as an access point for adult learning. Some communities and individuals prefer subject experts to lead whatever class they would want to take. This could be because the speaker's expertise lends needed public credibility to the subject matter (e.g., having a veterinarian give a class on at-home animal first aid). Others simply fill a niche with an experience, subject specialty, hobby, or interest and demonstrate a wealth of knowledge that is normally not accessible to a public audience (e.g., someone sharing their experience on how they started a successful restaurant). For the speakers, presenting at the library is a way for some to share their passion, subtly market their business or skills, or network with a new audience. Finance, history, health, technology, education, crafts, for every adult interest, there is likely a local expert who may be glad of the opportunity to present to the public.

THINGS TO CONSIDER

Whether looking locally or further afield, there are some firm pieces of information that the library should know before they contact a potential speaker. These include: topic, learning goals, budget, intended audience, the date, and the time. These are all questions that any potential presenter will need to know before they can ascertain if they are interested or able to partner with the library. Having firm answers to topic and learning goals also give speakers a framework in which to create their material. This can be important as an ambiguous request (e.g., "a program on health insurance for the elderly") can result in many possible programs, only some of which may fit in with the library's goals.

The starting point for any instructor search is the program topic. If the library is looking for a speaker on health insurance for the elderly, there are several possible options. An insurance company says that they can give a presentation on the different types of available health insurance. A healthcare facility billing specialist recommends a program on things to look out for with the most common type of insurance and common medical expenses for the elderly. A social worker who specializes in the subject recommends a demonstration specifically on how to navigate the official website and sign up online. A professor who teaches about the subject in the local college suggests a lecture on the history and future impact of the new healthcare laws. Any of these options had the potential to give a program in the desired topic, but the end choice depends on the learning goals that the library wants for the class. If the end goal for the class is that people know more about their choices, then the health insurance specialist may be the best choice. If the goal is that people see how to access information and a demonstration of how they will have to sign up, then the social worker is the best option.

Budget and programming times are often two of the make-or-break considerations for many libraries when considering a speaker. Some experts make part of their income from speaking or giving classes in their subject. Others may be part of a company, institution, or interest group that considers such opportunities part of their overall endeavor, a marketing strategy, or a matter of public service and therefore may not charge a fee. Outside speakers may or may not request a fee, but good practice generally dictates that the library at least offers an honorarium when possible that covers travel expenses. For many libraries this means that it is only possible to engage local talent. Scheduling is another factor and the speaker choice may be contingent on them being able to teach on specific dates and times. Other libraries may have more leeway and be able to offer several dates and time from which the speaker can choose. Most library programming is planned months in advance, if not more, to accommodate room schedules, staff schedules, and marketing deadlines, making these negotiations a necessity long before the program occurs.

FINDING A SPEAKER

There are several avenues to consider when searching for an outside speaker that include community members, local businesses, interest groups, referrals, and even organized speaker's bureaus. Library patrons and community members may be a great source of information regarding potential speakers. Some individuals and businesses will themselves approach the library about giving a program. Even if the library cannot accommodate the class or program they originally had in mind, they may be willing to modify their program to fit within library interests and goals. Recommendations from patrons can come in the form of another program that they've attended at some other function, such as a business or social event and may only require going to that entity's website to view the speaker information. Some libraries have a section on their website that solicits program ideas and speaker recommendations, while others build it into existing program evaluation forms.

Local businesses can sometimes be viewed as built-in interest groups that have a vested interest in community engagement. Many business owners or management teams may not naturally think about partnering with the library for programs but are often open to the idea when the process and potential benefits are laid before them. Some successful partnerships have included restaurants giving cooking lessons and start-up stories, sewing lessons from the local craft shop, calligraphy lessons from a stationary store, taking care of houseplants from the local nursery, and many more. These experiences give people a chance to get to know the businesses, the people behind the scenes, how they work, a little of what they know, and often a reminder of why they pay someone else to do whatever it is they just tried to do. The business advertises their expertise, their business in general, and expands their community engagement.

Pairing a topic with the terms "interest group" or "association" in an Internet search can reveal a variety of speaker resources in any given geographic location. These groups may offices, chapters, and conferences, or they may be smaller enclaves that only exist as a website with a calendar when they meet. Most have some form of contact information that helps to start the process of finding a speaker. One library, after learning about how ham radio operators all around the country aided during recent disasters, searched "ham radio" and "local chapter" along with the county name. There turned out to be several clubs, but the first one contacted was more than willing to give a free program on how their "hobby" had helped in multiple disaster relief efforts. The lecture program turned into regular ham radio class and testing session that has gotten more than twenty individuals their ham radio license (the author included).

State agencies, local government, and public and private organizations often maintain speaker's bureaus or lists of subject or skill-acknowledged speakers on a variety of topics. These can be curated and maintained by any organization or association but are usually topic-specific. In the library world, the American Library Association maintains a speaker's bureau, as does the Public Library Association (ALA, n.d.; PLA 2018). Many states and large cities maintain a humanities speaker's bureau that has specialists in a variety of current topics such as history, social justice, and cultural interests that might be of interest to the public. Any subject or topic with a large enough following will often have associated organizations and interest groups. If the topic and the organizations have been around long enough, a search using these terms along with the terms "request a speaker" or "speakers bureau" will often garner a ready-made list of recommended speakers.

IT'S NOT *JUST* WHAT THEY KNOW . . .

In the search to find someone topically knowledgeable, available for program dates, affordable, and interested in presenting at the library, it is important to remember that all that information does not mean that they will be any good at teaching. Despite their topic or how much the public recognizes that the person is not a library employee, they are recognized to be a representative of the library. This means that their appearance, their demeanor, and their ability to convey the promised information will be ultimately reflective of the library as a learning institution. The library can make requests at the outset as to dress, presentation style, how and if they take questions, and class format so that the potential presenter has the choice to turn down either the options or the gig.

There should be some expected differences between a professional speaker (e.g., a professor or someone from a speaker's bureau) and an amateur speaker (e.g., a local business person) in terms of poise, ease of speaking, and engagement of the audience. Some amateurs are natural presenters and teachers, but any speaker should be interested in the subject and interested that people learn. For some libraries, the recommendation source, such as a speaker's bureau or another library who engaged the speaker's services, is a good enough indicator of their abilities. Others might rely on reviews given by previous engagements or trust their status as a "professional speaker." Many speakers may be willing to share recorded examples of their work or examples of their presentations. If a meeting in person is possible, the library can request that the speaker give a short demonstration of their presentation to ascertain appearance, demeanor, and teaching style. This may even mentally help first-time presenters, such as local business owners or interest groups, so that they better understand what is expected of them and have a chance to view the teaching space. Library staff may decide to act as class aides or program monitors during a class if there is any question as to the speaker's ability to engage the audience, keep on schedule, or deal with any interruptions. Even if they are up to the task themselves, having a member of staff in the room can help answer questions that arise as to associated library resources, future library events, and general housekeeping needs that might come up.

THE FINE PRINT

A contract or other form of signed agreement should be employed with all outside instructors. The contract terms depend on the parties involved and the situation but helps ensure that all parties are clear on expectations and responsibilities. This is for the benefit of both parties; the library agrees to the instructor's fee (if applicable), the reproduction of handouts, class setup, and the advertisement of the course. The instructor agrees to dates, times, learning objectives, class format, content creation, and a professional behavior model. Some libraries leave the behavior control of the class to the visiting instructor and staff may not even be present during the program. Others maintain that library staff will address all technology and attendee behavioral issues. Templates and examples are available for this purpose all over the web using searches that use the terms "speaker contract" and "template." They are also available in the library databases that feature common legal forms such as *Legal Forms Library* or *Gale LegalForms*, but public libraries often need to conform to certain procedural processes, which depend on state and local laws before the creation of what is essentially a legal document. Library administration or local library agencies can help answer those questions and potentially even provide templates of their own for this purpose.

The instructor is responsible for themselves, the class process, the content, and for making sure that all possible considerations are made to maximize the learning potential of those who come to the library for classes and programs. An instructor's willingness to teach, a clear understanding of how to design and present information, good communication skills, and an understanding of adult learners will benefit both those who attend the class and the reputation of the library to the community.

BIBLIOGRAPHY

American Library Association (ALA). n.d. "ACRL Officers Speakers Bureau." http://www.ala.org/acrl/aboutacrl/directoryofleadership/chapters/officersspeakers.

Public Library Association (PLA). 2018. "PLA Speakers Bureau." http://www.ala.org/pla/about/workingwith/pla-speakers-bureau.

TWELVE

Overcoming Barriers

An important aspect in the study of how adults learn is the study of what makes them not participate in learning opportunities or to stop learning. These are referred to as learning barriers and are the internal or external factors that negatively affect a person's ability to learn. An awareness of these barriers allows teachers and institutions the chance to address them before a potential learner ever comes to or contacts the library. Researchers categorize these barriers into three categories (Falasca 2011, 583–89):

- Situational: things in the individual's personal life that interfere with learning
- Institutional: meaning library policies and procedures that prove a barrier
- Dispositional: the thoughts, feelings, beliefs, and perceptions of the learner

This chapter looks specifically at the different learning barriers adults might encounter with library instruction, and what the library and the instructor can do to overcome them or lessen their effect on a learner.

OVERCOMING PARTICIPATION BARRIERS

One of the largest barriers to learning at the library is the lack of knowledge that the opportunity exists. There are many reasons that adults in the community may not be aware of what the library has to offer in terms of physical and online resources, classes and programs, and personal instruction opportunities. This can frustrate many librarians who spend a lot of time, effort, and money analyzing their community in order to produce programs and buy materials that would immediately address their information needs, only to have expensive materials and databases sit unused or have classes unattended.

Depending on factors such as cost and staff resources, marketing efforts can utilize different outlets to advertise and promote library services and events. These might include traditional media, such as local newspapers, television, or radio stations. Local papers can run a library's calendar of events to make sure that all upcoming programs are available in one easy to access medium. Some libraries use special events, such as the summer reading program, a series of job seeker programs, or large author events to advertise on costly television spots. Sometimes local media will advertise library services without prompting or payment, if the event or the results create a large impact in the community. For example, this author's library was inundated with e-book instruction requests when a morning radio host raved about his experience at the library's Kindle class, having attended the previous evening.

Online marketing, such as using social media or online music streaming services such as Pandora or iHeart radio, can reach a different audience than traditional means. Facebook, Pinterest, Twitter, Instagram, and other social media platforms offer libraries the opportunity to instantly post updates, calendars, pictures, videos, program and service reminders, and links to other learning opportunities at any time. The demographics of the community should not only guide what learning opportunity the library provides but also determine which marketing approach and outlets would be more effective.

Some libraries use bookmarks and mailers or place or post flyers, posters, or other highly visible marketing material in high-traffic areas in the community to reach people where they live their daily lives. The marketing and promotion of library services and programs are so important to public perception and overall library use that library associations have resources and training opportunities built in to their sites and available to help libraries maximize their marketing efforts (ALA 2006; PLA 2018). These include a variety of webinars and articles that teach the basics of marketing library products as well as links to content creation sites such as Canva.com, a free online design program, and the *Libraries Transform* site, an ALA initiative that offers access to a variety of print and web templates such as posters, bookmarks, and web graphics for libraries to use in their local marketing efforts (ALA 2017).

One way to both inform and instruct potential users about what the library has to help them is for the librarian to leave the physical building, taking his or her skills and resources around the community (Shumaker 2009, 240). With this approach to service, sometimes referred to as embedded librarianship, librarians can go on location to local makerspaces, schools, community centers, or businesses to offer information and instruction at the actual point of need. This expands some of the more traditional forms of outreach, such as material delivery to eldercare facilities, schools, or bookmobiles and brings the library directly to the public.

Libraries can partner with other entities to address specific needs and interests in the community. A partnership with local health organizations, such as hospitals or clinics, can be used to teach health information literacy. This may mean that medical experts give programs at the library about what to eat if you have diabetes or how to help family members who have been diagnosed with cancer, or it could mean that librarians give programs at off-site locations on how to find health information and resources. Partnerships with government agencies, local to federal, can cover a variety of civil issues such as poverty and economics, financial literacy, business growth, literacy endeavors, or citizenship. One example of this is the *Civics and Citizenship Toolkit*, a program and collection development resource for libraries to enhance their offerings for immigrant populations made available by the U.S. Department of Homeland Security's department for U.S. Citizenship and Immigration services (Homeland Security 2011).

You may wish to begin by seeking permission to attend the meetings of local groups, organizations, or councils, perhaps offering short presentations as a way to show how the library is relevant to community interests. Local business groups (e.g., the Chamber of Commerce or a small business association) may be interested in business resources (e.g., notary services or distributor and manufacturing lists) that they can use to cut costs. A local craft group (e.g., a quilters association or knitting club) may benefit from knowing that library rooms are available for their group to use as well as what materials are in the library that pertain to their interests. These interactions can also be used to solicit sources for a library program, such as with a local historical reenactment group. Besides the library holding historical information that they might find useful for their hobby, they could present programs on how to get started in reenacting, what food and clothing looked like during a certain era, or how to design a costume. This kind of "overt purposefulness" along with keen observation and good communication with those in the community will increase awareness on the part of the library as to what people and user groups really need and want (Dewey 2004, 6).

OVERCOMING LEARNING BARRIERS

Even if someone knows that help and information are available at the library, there may be other barriers that prevent them from utilizing library resources. These may be real issues or imagined, but the reality is that they still impact an individual's ability and will to participate and learn.

Institutional barriers refer to policies or procedures of the library that cause individuals to not come to the library, use materials, or engage library services. For example, class or program times and places can be deterrents, especially if they are always grouped around a certain day or time, which will always exclude certain members of the population. If you are getting complaints about your program logistics, consider offering the same program repeatedly at various times. If this is not possible, consider embedding links to online resources and tutorials or one-on-one instructional opportunities on the same webpage as the event information or registration page. This can connect those ready to learn to alternate learning opportunities.

Another common institutional barrier can occur when someone needs a library card in order to participate in classes or even use in-house materials. Libraries may have that prerequisite for classes as a means to offer a value-added service to library constituents. Of course, many times it isn't a requirement, but a simple misunderstanding on the part of the would-be participant, either because of past experience elsewhere or the lack of clarity on a registration site can prompt confusion and disengagement. Non-library users may even see a library card as a necessary prerequisite to talk to staff, which is why it is so important that library staff pay attention and offer help to those who exhibit confused or unsure body language.

However, not being a card-holder in good standing usually is a real and potential barrier in regards to online services and library databases due to usage agreements with vendors. Some libraries address this by offering e-Cards or temporary library card numbers that allow non-card-holders to use online products and services for a certain length of time. Some libraries who have done away with "no talking" policies or the like have actually lost library users, since they no longer see the library as a place conducive to reflection, study, and learning. Other, more common deterrents are the lack of parking, no-children policies in classes, and especially the demeanor of the staff, which can all serve as barriers to someone seeking information or instruction.

Situational barriers occur when personal circumstances affect someone's ability to participate or learn. Employment, family roles and responsibilities, transportation realities, health issues, finances, and other considerations that are unique to each individual have a direct impact on motivation and ability to engage or retain information. You've probably heard patrons say "It's too far away," "I don't have time," "I don't have a ride," or "We just go for the kids." These are all examples of situational rationales that patrons use to justify not utilizing library services. Some of these are not problems that the library can address, but others may be a matter of the library maximizing timing and location, especially if the patron is already in the library. An example would be for an adult or reference librarian to engage parents waiting outside of a story-time room while their children are in a program. Here's an example of a librarian giving a short offer of specific library goods and services:

> Hi Folks. I'm from the reference section and, while you're waiting, I wanted to see if anyone here is a business owner or wants to be. I have some information here that shows you how to get free legal forms, helps you get marketing information, and how to access some useful business tutorials from our site. There's information in here about some upcoming classes that may interest you as well. I know you're all busy right now, but if you have any questions, just give us a call anytime or come to the reference desk and we'll help. Feel free to take more than one if you know someone who might like the information as well.

The librarian in this example sought to address the specific needs and interests of a particular group—that of current or would-be entrepreneurs—with passive instructional material, active instruction, and the promise to help if needed. Situationally, this group of parents was prioritizing their time toward their children by bringing them to a library event. This information may have been passively available nearby, but one short, friendly spiel can educate an entire group on previously unknown, and very useful, tools and resources. The best way a library can combat situational barriers is to show how the time, effort, and resources spent by the patron are worth the effort by speaking to their particular need.

Dispositional barriers are the internal factors, such as stress, low self-esteem, low motivation, and fear of failure that many people suffer; and these issues may not be apparent to you. A person may be physically present, having overcome situational and institutional barriers to be there, but their mental state, emotions, and beliefs interfere with their ability to learn. Some individuals are trepidatious of any situation that puts them back to a "student" role because of a negative connotation with formal education. Others who are there because they have an external motivator and they "have to" be there may feel resentment at the necessity or inconvenience. Simply put, negative emotions and thoughts about anything, whether it's about the material or not, make learning and recall more difficult.

Many public librarians around the country saw proof of this when the need to sign up online for the Affordable Care Act brought many with no technology experience or Internet access into the library for access and assistance (Real et al. 2015, 1–5). In many ways, individuals indicated a readiness to learn: they knew why they needed the information, many had already tried it themselves with various degrees of success and failure, and they were taking steps to address their information need by asking for librarian assistance or attending a class. The disposition of many, though, was one of anxiety, fear, and frustration. Some feared the potential financial and legal consequences of doing it wrong. Others were unfamiliar with technology and now had to quickly gain new skills and knowledge in order to perform a now mandatory function. Others were simply resentful of the necessity and change from their normal routine. Regardless of the reason, the vast array of librarians who assist individuals in any learning situation can attest to how negative disposition creates a hurdle for both of them to overcome for learning to occur.

Although dispositional barriers are sometimes identified as the most difficult barriers to address, since issues are internal and not directly identifiable unless they are overtly shared, there are several things that you as the instructor can do to help overcome these obstacles. A *safe environment*, or a situation free of judgement but full of support, is an essential first step. Specifically, this means avoiding acting in a way that demonstrates surprise or derision over someone's lack of ability or knowledge. It may seem like a given, but to a person who is nervous, self-conscious, or frustrated, anything but a positive and supportive attitude on the part of the teacher may exacerbate their negative state. This doesn't mean that the instructor has to either have or fake a chirpy, Pollyanna demeanor or issue false praise, but it does mean that they have to foster learner empathy, a "want to help" attitude, a real desire for the student to get what they need, and the ability to offer positive feedback (Klein, Noe, and Wang 2006, 671–74). Positive feedback can be simple verbal phrases, such as "good job," "good question," or "just like that. You've got it." Positive nonverbal feedback can be looking and smiling at the person when they ask a question or a nod or a thumbs-up when checking their work during an activity. The instructor's positive demeanor and enthusiasm will set the tone for the rest of the class and help create the safe environment needed for those who might come with dispositional barriers.

Basic *comfort considerations*, such as the students' ability to see or hear the material or the speaker, and the perceived relevance of the material will also help alleviate mental barriers. This is true in both passive and active learning situations (e.g., people whose passive library experience includes bad lighting, heating or cooling issues, confusing catalogs, and other distractions will find it harder to stay motivated to resolve their learning need). Minimizing distractions and emphasizing the connection between what they want to accomplish with what they'll learn will help keep them motivated and increase retention of the material (Sharit and Czaja 2018, 8–9). This means instead of simply telling the online sociology student about the social issues database by saying "Here's something that can help you," a librarian can say "Here's *how* this can help you." They can then draw a direct line to how it applies to them by showing how the site presents both sides of an argument for a variety of controversial social issues. This not-too-subtle reminder of why the students should exert the time and effort may help motivate them to focus on the material and the process and help them overcome mental barriers (Ronan 2017, 255).

In order to counter any of these barriers during instruction, it's important for you to consciously listen to what people say and to look for physical signs of confusion, frustration, discomfort, and apathy. Nonverbal signs of these negative feelings can include scowling, grimaces, eye-rolling, crossed arms, finger-tapping, and general fidgeting, which all communicate that they are either not mentally engaged or having some sort of problem with the material. Asking questions of the learner can also help the instructor determine their level of understanding and ability. Practice explaining processes and information in different ways or have more than one way to teach a subject or point of information (see chapter 5). One illustration used for this purpose was when someone in a basic computer class exhibited confusion as to what a browser was and why there were different types. The instructor asked if everyone had cable TV, then after an affirmative, pointed out that while everyone had a different cable company, they were all watching the same networks (i.e., the cable company was just the entrance to the channels, like browsers were the entrance to get online). Using concrete illustrations, multiple modes of presentation, asking open-ended questions, and making sure to break large concepts and processes into smaller steps is an effective way to teach to the most people and consistently address cognitive barriers.

Adults have many external and internal factors that affect if, when, and how they'll utilize the library as a learning resource. A conscious effort on the part of libraries and staff to minimize and help people overcome barriers to participation and learning can result in effective teaching opportunities and a long-lasting relationship with those in their communities.

BIBLIOGRAPHY

American Library Association (ALA). 2006. *Communications & Marketing Office*, July 24. http://www.ala.org/aboutala/offices/cmo.

American Library Association (ALA). 2017. "Toolkit." *Libraries Transform Campaign*. http://www.ilovelibraries.org/librariestransform/toolkit.

Dewey, Barbara I. 2004. "The Embedded Librarian: Strategic Campus Collaborations." *Resource Sharing & Information Networks* 17 (1–2): 5–17.

Falasca, Marina. 2011. "Barriers to Adult Learning: Bridging the Gap." *Australian Journal of Adult Learning* 51 (3): 583–90.

Homeland Security. 2010. *Civics and Citizenship Toolkit: A Collection of Educational Resources for Immigrants*. Washington, D.C.: U.S. Government Printing Office.

Klein, Howard J., Raymond A. Noe, and Chongwei Wang. 2006. "Motivation to Learn and Course Outcomes: The Impact of Delivery Mode, Learning Goal Orientation, and Perceived Barriers and Enablers." *Personnel Psychology* 59 (3): 665–702.

Public Library Association (PLA). 2018. "PR Resources." *Professional Tools*, July 30, 2018. http://www.ala.org/pla/resources/tools/public-relations-marketing/pr-resources.

Real, Brian, Abigail J. McDermott, John Carlo Bertot, and Paul T. Jaeger. 2015. "Digital Inclusion and the Affordable Care Act: Public

Libraries, Politics, Policy, and Enrollment in 'Obamacare'." *Public Library Quarterly* 34 (1): 1–22.

Ronan, C. Bonnie. 2017. "Will They Actually Use It? Teaching Effectively to Ensure Action on Patient Education." *Journal of Consumer Health on the Internet* 21 (3): 251–62.

Sharit, Joseph, and Sara J. Czaja. 2018. "Overcoming Older Adult Barriers to Learning through an Understanding of Perspectives on Human Information Processing." *Journal of Applied Gerontology* 18 (1): 1–18.

Shumaker, David. 2009. "Who Let the librarians Out? Embedded Librarianship and the Library Manager." *Reference & User Services Quarterly* 48 (3): 239–42.

THIRTEEN

Assessment Tools and Strategies

Patron counts, circulation statistics, database usage—libraries tradition-ally measure a variety of statistics in regard to their services and resources. Assessments tangibly communicate the outcomes and impact of library efforts to the community, library administration, library employees, and any stakeholder or party who has an interest in how money, time, and effort is expended by the library. These are also valuable evaluation tools for departments and libraries to use for products, services, and programs with an aim toward improvement, change, and ensuring that efforts meet with library missions and goals. Measuring and assessing library efforts in teaching adults makes sure that current and future efforts are making the most of knowledge, skills, and resources so that every possible teaching and learning interaction has the most impact for individuals, the commu-nity, and the library.

THE NECESSITY OF ASSESSMENT

Any institution that receives money (e.g., taxes or grants) or other mate-rial (e.g., in the case of a library, a building, computers, or books) has the responsibility to justify or report activities and expenditures to the stake-holders. Library stakeholders are a person, group, or entity that has decision-making capabilities regarding the library or its resources. Public libraries, depending on where they are located, may have a variety of stakeholder sources in the federal, state, county, and local governments, from which they might receive operating and resource funding (Cassell and Hiremath 2006, 316). The Institute of Museum and Library Services (IMLS) is one such entity, and it offers a webpage of helpful evaluation tips and resources as well as having very specific requirements for assessment as part of the application material for most programs and grant opportunities (IMLS 2018). Other stakeholders may include library branches, library departments, or consortiums that the library may be a part, which might share or compete for resources. Non-library partners, such as corporations that grant money or materials, schools that share space or materials, or local associations that could offer expertise, often want tangible data that helps prove to them and their stakeholders that the partnership is worth the effort. These relationships are often contingent on the library agreeing to report back with specific data, such as usage statistics, program numbers, or other, pre-agreed upon information before the library can receive help in the form of funds, materials, or partnerships.

Each public library has its own vision statement, mission statement, or set of goals that explicitly states the purpose of the library and what it plans to contribute to individuals and the community. Ensuring that library programs and services, such as adult learning activities, fit within and support these statements and goals are a way to justify the expenditure of time, money, and effort. The library must also assess and measure their use of resources, programming, services, and staffing for its own internal decisions, such as program budget allotments, room space, resource allocation, and staffing and hiring decisions. These measurements help librarians, managers, departments, and library administration make important decisions about what materials, services, programs, and in some cases which staff, continue to be part of library offerings.

The American Library Association (2018), the Public Library Association (2016), and the Reference and User Services Association (2008) are just a few library associations that list adult instruction as an important objective of library services, products, and programs. *Project Outcome*, a free online assessment toolkit provided by the PLA, lists seven services that the public, as well stakeholders, view as meaningful and valuable (Teasdale 2015). These include civic and community engagement, digital inclusion, early childhood literacy, economic development, education and lifelong learning, job skills, and summer reading or the encouragement of leisure reading. Notice that all but one of these can be articulated as adult learning endeavors and have been touched on in some form in this work as an opportunity for either passive, one-on-one, or group instruction.

WHAT TO MEASURE

How a program or service is assessed should automatically be built into it from the beginning as part of the design and planning process (see the ADDIE model in chapter 7). What is assessed, or the questions that the library wants to discover, may look different depending on the product, audience, and instructor, since the things to measure and assess will be based on the topic and the goal (Okobi 2014, 73–74). Some questions have to do with the content, the library space, the class format, and the instructors themselves. Many of these are often the only way that instructors, who might never have a staff member in the audience, get feedback on various aspects that have been covered in this work, such as their speaking or teaching skills, how they handle technology problems and behavior situations, their presentation of material, or their associated class material (e.g., handouts). Certain questions may be included in every program evaluation, such as impressions on the presenter's coherence or delivery skills, their knowledge of the subject, their interest in attendees, their handouts and presentation, how they answered questions, and whether the attendee felt that they "learned" anything. Other questions can be added to evaluations to reflect the varying expectations or goals that exist between different classes and programs.

Different learning environments result in different questions and means of measurement. Assessment of passive learning, which may include displays, material circulation, website access, or database use, may simply be a count of materials printed, circulation numbers, or site hits. Low numbers could mean that materials aren't being highlighted or marketed to the greatest advantage. To fix this, physical materials could be moved to a more high-traffic location, displays and brochure design could be reconsidered to better draw the eye, and web design could analyze the placement of links and promotions on the website to get better hits. Comment boxes in the library or by displays and online surveys can attempt to garner feedback on passive instruction so that the library doesn't rely on numbers alone and has the chance to take suggestions.

Service desks are a point of service that frequently result in requests for instruction, whether that is the designated location for that service or not. In order to avoid bouncing visitors from one desk to another, many libraries will perform a user-experience study that tracks the types of questions that are asked at different service desks in order to put services and appropriately skilled staff to where people are naturally gravitating. If the study shows that most instruction-related requests are asked at a certain desk, a desk labeled "computer" versus "reference," for example, this may indicate that some change should maybe occur in signage, staff duties, or staff training so that it fits user expectations.

One-on-one instruction, in person or virtual, necessitates that the staff keep count of the number of interactions if they wish to prove how often these instances occur in comparison to general reference questions. Staff can also evaluate the transaction itself, by either observation or directly asking the patron questions. An observation can be that the patron repeats the steps, such as a database query or downloading an e-book, without additional help, therefore demonstrating that they "learned" from the brief instruction session. It can also be a direct observation of their attitude and body language. Do they appear more confident or satisfied or do they appear doubtful and frustrated? Follow-up questions should naturally be a part of any reference interview and are reflective of the patron's perception of the instructional interaction. These may include familiar phrases such as "Did that answer your question?," "Do you think you can do this on your own (or at home)?," and "Try it on your own while I'm here so that we know you've got it." These are all diagnostic phrases that help staff determine where the person is in their knowledge and skills and how they feel about the process.

In business or any competitive endeavor, it doesn't matter what someone says or what "everyone knows" to be true. Anecdotal evidence is generally not as powerful as tangible data. Assessments and evaluations are the quantifiable evidence that things have a purpose, serve a particular use, and have value (Powers 2014, 157). This means that if a program or service says that it will result in "X" knowledge or skills, there should be a way to evaluate if that occurred. Because the goals and purpose of each endeavor might be different, some of the questions should be different in order to evaluate its success. For example, the evaluation of a follow-along painting class focuses on the social and entertainment factor, while the evaluation of a class on how to change your own oil focuses on whether people feel like they know what they're doing when they go home. The art class could simply ask, "Did you have fun?," since that was listed as one of the goals in the class description. The oil change class could ask, "Do you feel confident in your ability to change your own oil?," since that's what the program promised. Adding a line that asks, "Is there anything you would change for future classes?," is an excellent way to get insightful feedback on issues that the class or evaluation creator may not have even considered. All the answers, whether they're generic or specific, can be used to reflect and improve on future library efforts.

MEASURING THE OUTCOME AND IMPACT OF INSTRUCTION

Outcomes and impacts are the result of library efforts and can be measured against missions, goals, patron satisfaction, and the accumulative effect on individuals and the community (Matthew 2015, 211–12; Powers 2014, 149–52; RUSA 2008). One study suggests that there are four main types of outcomes that can be derived from library services and programs (Streatfield and Markless 2012, 80). The first is the *effect*, or whether there was a change in someone's attitude or perception and if they were satisfied with the experience. An example of measuring this for instruction would be to survey participants after a presentation that highlighted someone's personal history, such as a Vietnam veteran's experience with the draft, their time overseas, and then coming home to a derisive public. Attendees may have had a certain perception of that war or opinions about its participants based on their own personal experience or their learning about it in history that could have been altered or expanded upon based on the presentation. Questions on the evaluation can be worded to point out how it may have affected someone's perceptions and attitudes, such as "Did this presentation introduce new information about the Vietnam War and its participants?" This may make them acknowledge, for example, that they were not aware of the emotional toil of the draft and what it did to families. These types of reflective questions help participants connect how they have, in fact, gained in experience, knowledge, and potentially empathy by attending such programs.

The second type of outcome is *behavioral*, where someone's behavior is modified because of what they have learned or experienced. Examples of this could include a smartphone class that changes how someone interacts with an unwanted call, a class on buying your first home that now has a patron consistently monitoring their credit report, or a program on fake news that has changed how someone listens to and processes news reports. Some behaviors are immediately modified as soon as the patron has the rationale and the new information. For others, it's a matter of acquiring a new habit or mindset that began with the library program or instruction interaction. One large behavior change that has occurred for many patrons is using their personal device to borrow e-books and e-audiobooks instead of buying them. Many individuals who had the (potentially expensive) habit of simply going to the shop feature of their device learned from friends, family, passive advertisement, or direct library marketing efforts that they could get the same materials from the library for free. They had to overcome the ease-of-use habit of simply buying materials and build a new behavior of trying the library e-book applications first. Libraries are full of stories from patrons on how information or skills learned from a library program, book, or class changed their life in some short or long-term way. Because it can take longer than a single class session to comprehend the behavioral impact of instruction, libraries may wish to solicit experiences and personal outcomes and impacts from patrons using online or in-house (non-program-related) surveys, focus groups, interviews, or by requesting stories via social media.

Knowledge-based outcomes can be seen when participants gain new information or understanding. This may translate to new skills, such as knowing how Boolean operators such as +, *xor,* and quotation marks can improve search engine results; or it can be a piece of information that broadens understanding and connects preexisting schemas, such as learning about language code-switching and the historical and cultural reason why some people say "ax" instead of "ask." Knowledge-based assessment can be trickier to assess in certain situations. If an attendee already knew the information, but was entertained and satisfied with the presentation, was it still successful? If the evaluation only asked if they learned something "new," then a "no" answer may seem detrimental, but if another question simply asked if they were satisfied or entertained by the session, then a "yes" proves that it was still a successful event for that participant. Someone may relish the opportunity to practice under supervision, even if they already "know" the information, such as a computer or software class. Others may have a negative connotation of the session because they did not learn anything "new" and therefore didn't "get anything" from the class or program. Clearly defined and descriptive program summaries help potential participants understand exactly what knowledge a class or program will provide, which can cull attendees who might feel they already know the information and therefore not benefit from the program.

The last suggested measure is *competence-based* outcomes, which refers to newly acquired information or skills that improve someone's ability, a.k.a. they become more competent at a task. Beginner, technology-based classes and one-on-ones are good examples of someone coming to a session and leaving the library with a marked difference in competency and skill level. This can happen at any level of a skill-based class, from someone learning in one session how to correctly use the left and right buttons on a mouse, to someone learning how to layer multiple lines of audio tracks on Apple's GarageBand. Bibliographic instruction, or teaching people how to use library goods and services, is another frequent competence-based outcome, since they have either learned how to perform a function such as place a book on hold, return an e-book, access a database, or check their account online . . . or they have not. The learner is the ultimate determiner of whether they are "competent," which is often demonstrated by someone leaving an instructor-perceived "successful" session doubtful of their ability to perform the same skills on their own (Newman 2012, 40–44). Measuring this outcome is then a combination of observing that they have successfully completed an action on their own and are of the opinion that they can repeat the action or skill independently.

Measuring the outcome and impact of adult learning and library-led instruction interactions can help ensure that libraries have the necessary tools to continue, improve, and potentially increase library efforts toward staff skills in adult learning and education as well as associated services, programs, or resources.

TOOLS FOR ASSESSMENT

A variety of methods for assessment of library instruction have been discussed in the previous paragraphs, including surveys, observation, counts, suggestion boxes, social media anecdotes, focus groups, and polls. While these tools can be created from scratch, a variety of online tools, templates, and assessment instruction exists to help libraries successfully create, manage, analyze, and utilize gathered information.

Project Outcome

Project Outcome, as mentioned earlier in the chapter, is a free online toolkit for public libraries that provides training and assessment resources, such as webinars and templates (www.projectoutcome.org). These tools are specifically geared toward helping libraries prove their value, or as they say, answer the question, "What good did we do?" (PLA 2016).

Their site gives libraries access to customized tools such as report templates, data analysis resources, and learning tools meant to help libraries evaluate programs and events. A resource page at https://www.projectout come.org/surveys-resources provides a variety of sections, such as a

"Getting Started" section with assessment tutorials and rationales as to why measuring outcomes is important for libraries. The "Surveys" section provides guidance in which type of survey might suit a library's needs, print-on-demand surveys for immediate use, and information on how to write original surveys. "Data Collection" contains step-by-step information on how to gather information into a usable product, best practices, tips for patron interactions, and other information that can provide guidance for those who are new to gathering data from the public. The section on "Data Analysis" contains interactive tutorials on how to make the most of data, how to analyze it, and how to turn raw data into a usable tool. "Taking Action" teaches users how to communicate assessment findings and use that information as a tool for library advocacy. Finally, the "From the Field" section provides on-demand webinars and allows users to see how other libraries have used these tools and resources to navigate assessment successfully for the purpose of library advocacy in their community. It also provides an opportunity for users to offer feedback to Project Outcome and even speak to other participants in a peer discussion forum. Libraries also can create their own surveys under the "Survey Management Tools" section, which is an easy, interactive program that can be used to create assessment tools specifically for a program or generic templates.

LibQUAL+

LibQUAL is an example of a fee-based online survey system that will create assessment tools for libraries and then analyze the data. It is a product offered by the Association of Research Library (ARL) that is built to measures patron's perceptions and expectation of the library in an effort to analyze library services, organizational resources, and best practices. More information about services can be found at http://www.libqual.org/about/about_lq/general_info.

ISO 16439

In 2014, the International Organization for Standardization (ISO) created ISO 16439, a guide standard for the measurement of library performances and value, in response to demand from library systems around the world on how to assess the impact of libraries around the world (Creaser 2018, 87–90). The standard calls for libraries to measure a variety of elements in order to determine performance and value, including resource inputs, outputs in the form of services, outcomes or effects of the library outputs, the impact on individuals or the community, and the value of these to stakeholders. The stated purpose of the standard is:

1. To aid in the strategic planning and the internal quality management of libraries.
2. To be used as a comparative tool for library impact over time as well as against similar libraries.
3. To help libraries promote their role and value to their constituents in terms of learning, research, education, culture, and in social and economic instances.
4. To support libraries in political endeavors that affect the services and goals of the library. (ISO 2014, 1)

The suggested methods of evaluation are *inferred evidence*, which generally refers to usage and attendance numbers, *solicited evidence*, which can be focus groups, surveys, interviews, or anecdotal evidence, and *observed evidence*, which refer to self-assessment or the recorded observations of staff (ISO 2014, 21–49). The full publication of the standard contains more than twenty pages of detailed suggestions and applications for the three methods of evaluation. Measured consistently, these can identify the short-, medium-, and long-term impact of the library on a community.

THE BENEFITS OF COLLABORATION AND SHARING

Collaboration with other librarians and other libraries provides another way to gain access to effective tools and methods of evaluation. Listservs, accessible through local or state associations as well as through larger national entities such as ALA and PLA, are a great place to simply ask, "Can someone share an evaluation template or method for an adult history program/tech class/job skill workshop that worked for you?" The responses are often numerous and generous with forms, materials, and rationales for that method of assessment. They can also represent different perspectives, given the different library goals and audiences. While it is generally understood that receiving such information is permission to use it, it benefits both parties to get explicit permission to reuse or modify any material or wording that is shared, such as "The XYZ Library gives the ABC Library permission to reuse and modify the attached documents." For the sender, this means checking with the appropriate library authority that they have permission to share their library's material. "Don't reinvent the wheel" in terms of evaluation tools and methods is an axiom that can save staff and libraries a lot of time, effort, and potentially money.

Evaluation and assessment are tools that libraries use to prove or disprove that the program or service is relatable to library goals and missions. It should be a diagnostic tool that helps uncover problems such as staff skills, design flaws, or implementation weaknesses (Powers 2014, 157–58). It can also be diagnostic in that it tells the library what is working and why. Besides revealing findings to the library, these measurements also communicate the efforts and the value of library services to individual users, the community in general, and other library stakeholders. This type of information can be extrapolated to similar efforts and help streamline processes and training and can be used to create a reusable model (Matthews 2015, 217).

BIBLIOGRAPHY

American Library Association (ALA). 2018. "Library Instruction Round Table (LIRT)." *Library Instruction Roundtable*. http://www.ala.org/rt/lirt.

Amosford, John. 2007. "Assessing Generic Learning Outcomes in Public Lending Libraries." *Performance Measurement and Metrics* 8 (2): 127–36.

Association of Research Libraries. n.d. "General Information: What Is LibQUAL+?" *LibQUAL+: Charting Library Service Quality*. http://www.libqual.org/about/about_lq/general_info.

Cassell, Kay Ann, and Uma Hiremath. 2006. "Assessing and Improving Reference Services." In *Reference and Information Services in the 21st Century: An Introduction*, 315–35. New York: Neal-Schuman.

Creaser, Claire. 2018. "Assessing the Impact of Libraries—the Role of ISO 16439." *Information and Learning Science* 119 (1–2): 87–93. https://doi.org/10.1108/ILS-05-2017-0037.

Institution of Museum and Library Services (IMLS). 2018. "Evaluation Resources." *Research and Evaluation*. https://www.imls.gov/research-evaluation/evaluation-resources.

International Organization for Standardization (ISO). 2014. "Information and Documentation—Methods and Procedures for Assessing the Impact of Libraries." *ISO/DIS Standard 16439*. http://produccion-uc.bc.uc.edu.ve/programas/doc/conmuta/udo/ISO16439-2014.pdf.

Matthews, Joseph. 2015. "Assessing Outcomes and Values: It's All a Matter of Perspective." *Performance Measurement and Metrics* 16 (3): 211–33.

Newman, Michael. 2012. "Calling Transformative Learning into Question: Some Mutinous Thoughts." *Adult Education Quarterly* 62 (1): 36–55.

Okobi, Elsie A., and Rogers Halliday. 2014. "Assessment of Adult Services." In *Library Services for Adults in the 21st Century*, 73–96. Santa Barbara, CA: Libraries Unlimited.

Powers, Amanda Clay. 2014. "The Value of Reference Services: Using Assessment to Chart the Future." In *Reimagining Reference in the 21st Century*, edited by David A. Tyckoson and John G. Dove, 149–59. West Lafayette, IN: Purdue University Press.

Public Library Association (PLA). n.d. "Project Outcome." https://www.projectoutcome.org/.

Public Library Association (PLA). n.d. "Resources." *Project Outcome.* https://www.projectoutcome.org/surveys-resources.

Public Library Association (PLA). 2016. "Performance Measurement." *American Library Association.* http://www.ala.org/pla/initiatives/performancemeasurement.

Reference and User Services Association (RUSA). 2008. "Measuring and Assessing Reference Services and Resources: A Guide." *American Library Association.* http://www.ala.org/rusa/sections/rss/rsssection/rsscomm/evaluationofref/measrefguide.

Streatfield, David, and Sharon Markless. 2012. "Success Criteria and Impact Indicators: How You Know You Making a Difference." In *Evaluating the Impact of Your Library*, 79–104. London: Facet Publishing.

Teasdale, Rebecca. 2015. "Project Outcome Launch—Seven Surveys to Measure Impact." *Public Libraries Online.* http://publiclibrariesonline.org/2015/05/project-outcome-launch-seven-surveys-to-measure-impact/.

Index

About the Author

Jessica A. Curtis is an adult reference librarian at the Westerville Public Library in Ohio as well as a graduate instructor for the Kent State University Library iSchool. She is an active member and frequent presenter for the Ohio Library Council. She specializes in creating user-friendly classes for emerging technology and library services. She holds a BA from the Ohio State University and an MLIS from Kent State University.